vegetarian

gourmet

cookery

by alan hooker

Edited By

HELEN MORROW

Illustrated By

SARA RAFFETTO

DEDICATED TO VEGETARIANS EVERYWHERE

First Printing, November, 1970
Second Printing, January, 1971
Third Printing, May, 1971

PUBLISHED BY 101 PRODUCTIONS
79 Liberty Street, San Francisco, California 94110

contents

introduction

"There's no sauce in the world
like hunger."   —Cervantes

At the moment of birth a problem
is created which has to be faced
every day as long as one lives.
That problem is one's
relationship to the environment.
The infant solves the problem by
feeding and thus conditions
himself from the beginning with
the idea that when one is in
trouble—or in a strange situation
—and can think of nothing else
to do, one eats. In one form or
another this idea haunts us all
the days of our lives.

Some people use other than
physical food to assuage their
hunger—money, sex, social status,
etc., but still the simplest
comfort is palatable food.
There may be such a thing as
going beyond this eternal sense
of hunger to another level of
our being which does not
hunger, but this journey is
not taken by many people.

Rather than just eating
something to satisfy the pangs
of hunger, we can become more
perceptive about food. This may
have unanticipated repercussions,
for such sensitivity means a
deepening of our awareness of

all that surrounds us, thus providing more satisfaction from the environment.

When people come together who have not previously met they are a bit reserved; but when food is introduced there is an immediate change in the atmosphere. The power of the festive table begins to operate, bringing a feeling of gentleness and warmth. What I am trying to convey is that we have to begin somewhere to relate to the environment. How better than with food?

Why one decides no longer to eat meat is sometimes difficult to state. Every argument for a vegetarian diet can be met with an equally logical argument against. Years ago I read a book by Max Heindel in which he talked about the "oneness of all life." It made such sense to me that I stopped eating meat—for the first time. But gradually this philosophy slipped away. It was the time of the hectic Twenties, I was a traveling musician, and it was just too difficult to maintain a vegetarian diet.

After this period I lived for a time in Ohio and did the cooking for a community where we lived together. There was a market where chickens were killed for you as you waited. One day I stood there waiting for my chicken to be killed. Perhaps I was in a relaxed and receptive state, for when the chicken squawked for its life on being caught something within me screamed just as hard for my life. The man handed me a wrapped up dead chicken which I took home and put into the cooking pot. I served it on a platter, this dead chicken; but for me the transition to the word "meat" never took place. One cannot eat a "dead chicken" so, again I was not eating meat.

My wife Helen and I moved to the Ojai Valley in California and opened a boarding house where most of us were strict vegetarians. It became my job to invent new meatless entrees that would satisfy the non-vegetarian guests of the boarders. These new friends in turn invited their friends, and soon we were in real financial trouble. We had a begging bowl on the mantle, but found that the tradition of the bowl is not an American one, for it never contained enough money to pay our bills.

Eventually we opened a restaurant, The Ranch House. Although the restaurant did have a menu, guests began to ask, "Where is the meat?" In those days there were not enough patrons interested in a vegetarian diet to support us. The restaurant began to lose money, and so to survive (perhaps following nature's first law), I started experimenting with meat recipes and soon we were serving *toutes les viandes* at the Ranch House. The nightmares I had when I first began this transition are too horrible to recount.

During these years I have devised several hundred recipes, both vegetarian and

5

introduction

meat dishes, continually working to create something new. It is in the process of discovery that the fun of life comes, more than in what is discovered.

Personally I have again returned to a vegetarian diet. I think it is important to act in such a manner that guilt is not part of one's life. To eat meat and feel guilty is a horror, as I know only too well. To try and rationalize it is equally miserable. At any rate, once again I am a vegetarian, and though the Ranch House serves meat, it doesn't seem to bother me.

Perhaps interest is the key to the whole thing, I don't know; but I do know that the garden where we live is rife with things that excite me; new plants, new vegetables, new ways of making them happy in the garden, new ways of preparing them.

I hope this book will help you who use it and you who merely read it to provide for yourselves and others an adequate diet so you can live full vital lives, as you seek a better way to live in the world without having to resort to any type of violence—not even mental or emotional violence.

A sensitive approach to food may extend sensitivity almost without effort on our part, into other areas of our lives. Not only will our appreciation of the arts increase, but also we may be aided in practicing the most difficult and greatest art—that of friendly relationship to others. The art of getting along amicably with neighbors and friends requires true sensitivity, an awareness of all of man's hungers.

And so I think it useful to present this volume of vegetarian recipes that have been invented or adapted here at the Ranch House. Experimenting with them may bring out new facets of your understanding of food and people, and spur you on to do some inventing yourself. At least I hope so. Bon voyage on your food journeys!

A.H.
Ojai, California
June 4, 1970

7

herbs

HERBS HAVE A SPECIAL MAGIC

When one forgoes the stock pot as a source of flavoring, the herb garden acquires new meaning. A judicious use of herbs can change a dull dish into something of tongue-clicking interest. A new world of flavors opens with the use of those little leaves and plants. To the cook making a dietary change and worrying about missing the solid flavors of the flesh, combining herbs can be a challenge. So be creative and experiment. In fact, now the vegetable world takes on an entirely new aspect. The care that should always have been present when merely boiling a carrot, now becomes worthwhile because of the magic ingredient of new flavor. And see what herbs can do to ordinary cabbage, corn and tomatoes!

Let it be stated with emphasis that you should eliminate now from your cooking vocabulary two unfortunate terms: success and failure. There is no place for either of them in true experimentation. You cannot perform an experiment, if you are really interested in it, without learning something. I have been cooking for years and hardly a cooking day passes that I don't discover something new. Perhaps half of the things I try are not worth repeating; but from every experiment I learn more about what will or won't work.

I keep a notebook in which I write down what I have done, *after* I have done it. There is something about trying to record what you are doing while the experiment is going on that chokes off the fun and flow of creativity. Even if you forget one of the ingredients, when you come to the same stage again usually it will pop into your head. It is something like walking down a road and seeing landmarks as you go along.

ONIONS AND GARLIC

"A good cook begins with an onion," it is said. So let us begin our adventures with herbs the way a good cook should. One of the reasons, apart from flavor, for using any of the allium lily family is the power of penetration inherent in it. All the parts of a good dish need one central substance to bind them together, and the onion is most frequently used for this purpose. The onions in common use are Spanish and white, garlic, leeks, chives, shallots and scallions, the little green ones.

For most cooked dishes, onions are chopped fine and then cleared by cooking them in butter or oil. This is important, for just this much cooking makes the catalyst which binds the flavors. When clearing onions and/or garlic, the herbs you plan to use with them should be added only *after* the clearing. The heat would drive off some of the essential oils in the herbs, leaving what I call a hole in the flavor.

Used raw, onions keep more of their own particular characteristics and do not have this catalytic ability. They season like an herb, which is, of course, what they are.

Garlic. If the common onion is the most important seasoning (if such a distinction may be made), garlic is second. Many people use a garlic press, but I think this releases too much of the essential oils, which then evaporate. Garlic should be minced and cleared by cooking it in butter in a small covered pan until it looks transparent, but not browned. This may seem to be making a big thing out of something relatively unimportant, but I think you will find that it improves the flavor to treat the garlic in this way. Another good way to prepare the garlic cloves for seasoning is to pound them with salt in a mortar with a pestle.

Scallions, little green onions, are for foods that require a light flavoring. There is a multiplier onion that we grow to use as scallions,

which is excellent for this purpose. It grows like garlic, in clusters. It can be taken up and the buds separated, one of them replanted, and the process of growth begins again. This onion is easy to obtain from the nursery. Shallots grow in a similar manner.

Shallots, French bulbous onions, have a sweeter flavor. These two are not interchangeable. Bearnaise sauce, for instance, demands shallots as well as fresh French tarragon.

Leeks are like giant green onions, very sweet in flavor.

herbs

HERB COOKING MADE EASY

Now, about other herbs, those mysterious, often feared bits which hold such promise if only "someone would tell me how to use them!" Here's good news—it's easy! If one lacks the space to grow herbs, they are packaged and available in most stores. However, dried herbs do lose flavor from the evaporation of their essential oils. Buy them in small quantities.

In herb cooking, it is quite necessary to have a mortar and pestle. There are many types available: wood, glass and stoneware. We grind all of our herbs in this way.

First, let's divide herbs into some simple classifications for convenience: Sweet herbs, bitter herbs, fragrant herbs, tart herbs and peppery herbs. What do you want to flavor? And in what way? This will determine the herb combinations you will use. You need only to understand the properties of the important ones.

Sweet Herbs
Celery—Yes, it is an herb, and chervil is its strong brother.
Onion—Garlic is its strong brother.
Summer Savory—Winter savory is its strong brother.
Marjoram—Oregano is wild marjoram.
Basil—Anise is its strong brother.
Parsley—Coriander leaves, called Spanish parsley, is the stronger brother.

Bitter Herbs
Perhaps pungent is the better term. These include oregano, rosemary, thyme and sage.

Fragrant Herbs
Mint and peppermint, lemon verbena, costmary (delicate mint), tarragon (the sister to fennel).

Tart Herb: French sorrel

Peppery Herb
Watercress (the variety grown on dry ground is called overland cress.)

HERB BLENDS

There is no rule about herb mixtures. Herbs should be blended according to the individual preference for certain flavors imparted. Variety in dishes is obtained by varying the given amounts in any blend. However, some foods almost demand certain herbs: Tomato or cheese demands basil and eggs demand tarragon. Vegetables such as peas need only marjoram or mint, or both. Corn can nicely use thyme.

The two simplest combinations of herbs are, of course, onions and garlic; next, celery and parsley; then, marjoram or thyme. These last two, when added to onion and a touch of garlic, form a perfect combination of a sweet herb blend. The two classic methods of adding herbs to a dish are:

Aux Fines Herbes Finely chopped dried or fresh herbs added directly to the food and mixed throughout it.

Herb Bouquet (Bouquet Garni) Literally, a bouquet of fresh herbs tied together and immersed in a sauce or dish, and then removed before serving. If dried herbs are used, tie them in a cheesecloth bag. This is done to add the herb flavor without the herbs showing in the finished preparation.

At the Ranch House, we have developed some fines herbes mixtures that are called for in various recipes in this book. These are given in proportions so that they can be made up ahead of time and stored for use as needed:
All combinations are for dry herbs. They must not be portioned out by weight. Part refers to the size of the unit of measurement you are using: 1 tablespoon, 1 teaspoon, etc. Put the amount of salt or herb salt and the herbs you are going to use for your dish into a mortar and grind them together. The flavors will blend nicely and this mixture then can be added to the dish.

Herb Blend for Eggs
3 parts parsley.
1 part each: chervil, marjoram, tarragon, basil, chives.

Herb Blend for Salads
4 parts each: marjoram, basil, tarragon, parsley, chervil, celery, chives.
1 part each: lemon thyme, summer savory, costmary.

Herb Blend for Soups
2 parts each: thyme or summer savory, parsley, chervil, basil, sweet marjoram, celery or lovage leaves. 1 part each: sage, rosemary, dried ground lemon peel.

Herb Blend for Vegetables
1 part each: marjoram, basil, chervil, parsley, chives.
Pinch of: savory, thyme.

Savory Herb Blend
1 part each: basil, marjoram, celery tops, parsley, costmary, tarragon
Pinch of: savory, thyme.

Herb Salt There are several varieties of blended herb salt on the market. Our own herb salt and herb blends, which have become quite famous, are available from The Ranch House, 102 Besant Road, Ojai, California.

herbs

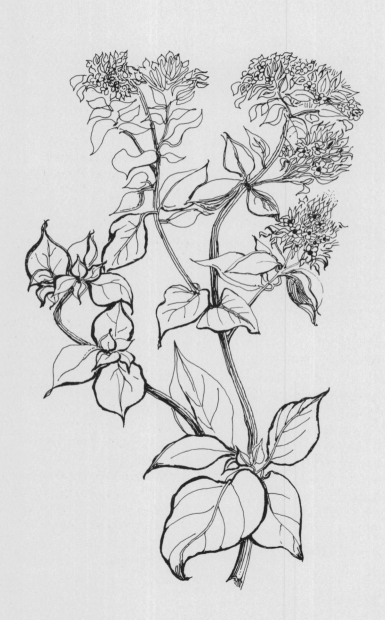

THE HERB GARDEN

A 3 by 3 foot plot of ground
at the kitchen door, or a box
with 8 pots, is most adequate
for the usual kitchen "bouquet
garni."
Here is the scheme:
 Marjoram   English Thyme
 Oregano Sage Mint Basil
 Summer Savory   Tarragon
The herbs shown above are partly
perennials, partly annuals.
Basil and summer savory are
annuals and to keep them growing
instead of going to seed, they
must be constantly cut back to
about 8 inches in height. All
blossoms and seeds must be
picked off. The cuttings of
leaves and blossoms may be laid
on wax paper on a flat surface
and dried for winter use.
In the culture of your herb
garden, experiment to see how
much sun the plants need. In
coastal areas they need full
sun, especially tarragon,
marjoram and thyme. Inland, a
little shade is acceptable. Good
drainage and fairly rich humus
soil speed growth. Keep the
plants picked back to encourage
branching.

THE SAUCE IS
THE MELODY

"Sauces are to cookery
what grammar is to language
and melody is to music"
—Careme and Soyer, Master Chefs

Home cooks are apt to think
that making many of the gourmet
sauces such as the famous
Bechamel requires a great
number of ingredients most of
which will be found only in the
kitchens of the famous restaurants
of the world. Our kitchen is a
small one and we do not always
have at hand this array of
ingredients. In vegetarian
cooking, I have often had to
improvise in order to get the
flavor and texture desired.

In my culinary thinking the
ingredients are often blended in
my mind, much as a pianist
practices his concert silently,
away from the piano. If you who
read this have never tried
mentally to concoct a dish, you
may be surprised to discover you
have the same ability. To
experiment, go where you won't
be interrupted and think of the
food you want to prepare, and
what you can do to improve
its flavor and texture.

I'd like to give you an example
of a simple sauce I made.
I visualized a small whole
carrot, steamed just enough to
remove the raw taste. Then I
imagined a crunchy texture and
to get it I chose poppy seed,
sesame seed, onion salt and
fresh peppercorns. I wanted
these flavors to blend together
more than they would when they
were whole, and I wanted an
accompanying flavor·that would
go in to marry all the other
ingredients. This was celery
seed. Then I went into the
kitchen and began mixing the
ingredients, always remembering
the intensity of each separate
one to achieve a proper balance.

On the supermarket shelves
today are substitutes for things
that had to be made from scratch
not too long ago. If a vegetable
broth is desired, a vegetable
cube can be dissolved to prepare
it. Granted these cubes are not
as good as the real thing, they
are a passable substitute and
they can broaden the scope of
any home cook. Also, modern
equipment such as a blender
makes it possible to prepare a
smooth sauce with so little
effort that there should be no
hesitance at all in attempting
even a complicated recipe.

Most of the sauces given here are
simple ones, although some of
them are famous in the cuisines
of famous chefs. This cookbook
is for ordinary people like myself
and I hope you do not mind
being included in this category.
Even though I love cooking I do
not want to spend endless hours
in the preparation process just
to follow some recipe devised
long before many of the present
day gadgets were invented.

sauces

SAUCE MORNAY

The secret of this sauce is the quality and age of the cheese. It must be a very strong variety such as a good cheddar, and well aged so that it will melt. The aging process breaks down the protein and makes it possible for the cheese to melt without getting stringy. Kraft has a sharp cheddar, packaged in a red foil wrapper, very good and available in most markets.

Heat in copper bottom pan so milk will not stick:
1 quart milk
1 bay leaf
(discard when milk is hot)
Melt in a small pan:
6 tablespoons butter
Blend well into butter to make a roux:
9-1/2 tablespoons flour
(be exact with this)
2-1/2 teaspoons herb salt
good dash white pepper
Add roux to heated milk, stirring constantly with wire whip until it thickens, then add and cook 1 minute:
1 egg yolk, mixed well in
1/4 cup coffee cream
14

When done, add and stir in, mixing thoroughly:
2-1/2 tablespoons sherry
3 ounces sharp cheddar, grated fine
1/4 teaspoon Worcestershire sauce
dash cayenne pepper
Then reheat, stirring constantly to blend all ingredients. This sauce is so good for so many uses that a large amount can be made and kept in the refrigerator for at least a week without spoiling. All that is necessary when you want to use some is to put it in a double boiler and reheat it.

RANCH HOUSE BECHAMEL SAUCE

Heat but do not boil (use no. 3 heat on electric stove, or very low flame on gas stove):
1 quart milk
1 bay leaf
Remove bay leaf when milk is hot. Heat in small saucepan:
6 tablespoons butter
Blend well:
9-1/2 tablespoons flour
2-1/2 teaspoons herb salt

1/16 teaspoon fresh ground pepper
Stir flour mixture into melted butter slowly, until it makes a thick paste, then add this mixture to heated milk and cook slowly, stirring with wire whip until thickened.

Mix together and add, and continue cooking until thick:
1 egg yolk
1/4 cup half-and-half cream
Remove mixture from fire and add:
3 tablespoons sherry (not dry)
Put small dots of butter on top of sauce to prevent scumming. Unless used immediately, cover and refrigerate when cool.

RICH CREAM SAUCE

Heat in copper bottom pan so it will not scorch:
1 pint whole milk
Melt:
3 tablespoons butter
Mix together and add to butter to make roux:
4-1/2 tablespoons white flour
1-1/4 teaspoon herb salt
dash white pepper

When milk is hot but not boiling, stir in flour and butter mixture. Do not have milk or roux too hot when mixing as this will cause lumps. Cook over low heat, stirring with wire whisk. When mixture begins to thicken add and stir in well:

1 tablespoon whipping cream or evaporated milk

Use this sauce in any recipe calling for a good cream sauce. It is wonderful thinned slightly and used to cream asparagus, peas, green beans or baby lima beans.

MUSHROOM GRAVY WITH SAVITA

Cook 2 minutes in saucepan:
2 tablespoons butter (browned)
1/2 pound sliced mushrooms
1/2 teaspoon herb salt
1/2 teaspoon savory herb blend
Add and cook until thick:
1 tablespoon savita, dissolved or 3 vegetable cubes
3 cups water
2 tablespoons cornstarch dissolved in cold water

FRESH MUSHROOM SAUCE

Cook until mushy:
2 tablespoons butter
1 clove garlic, minced
1/2 cup onions, sliced
1/8 teaspoon MSG (optional)
When onions start to get brown in color, add and cook until well done:
1/2 pound fresh mushrooms, sliced
1 tablespoon flour, mixed in
1/2 cup water
1/2 teaspoon lemon or lime juice
For a variation of this recipe, instead of adding the flour and citrus juice, use 1/2 cup of commercial sour cream and stir in well. The mushrooms should be cooked down to a good consistency for this, or the addition of the sour cream will make the mixture too thin. Served over omelettes or added to cooked rice, this recipe serves 4.

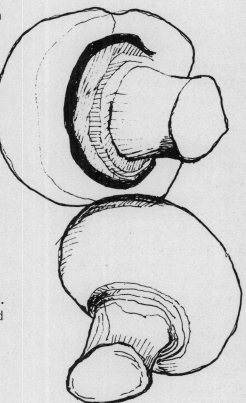

sauces

SPANISH SAUCE

Cook in kettle until vegetables
are done but not mushy:
4 cups onions, chopped coarse
3 cups celery, sliced
1 cup green peppers, cut coarse
1 cup mushrooms, sliced
(optional)
small can ripe olives, chopped
1 cup cooked tomatoes, mashed
2 vegetable cubes
1/2 tablespoon salt
1 bay leaf (discard when cooked)
1 clove garlic, minced
1/2 teaspoon tomato herb blend
When vegetables are done, add
and simmer 15 minutes:
3 small cans tomato paste
1 small can pimientos, chopped
This can be frozen and used
as needed, little by little.

ITALIAN SAUCE

Cook until clear:
4 tablespoons olive oil
2 cups onions, chopped fine
4 cloves garlic, minced
Add and boil slowly for 15
minutes:
2 large green peppers,
cut fine
16

4 bay leaves (discard when
cooked)
4 vegetable cubes
1 46-ounce can tomato juice
Pound in mortar and add:
1 teaspoon salt
1/2 teaspoon MSG (optional)
1/2 teaspoon rosemary
1/2 teaspoon thyme
1 teaspoon oregano
1 teaspoon basil
When vegetables are tender,
add and simmer for
30 minutes:
3 small cans tomato paste
This sauce can be frozen and
used as needed. Just chop
out desired amount without
defrosting the entire amount.

MUSHROOM SAUCE
FOR SPAGHETTI

Cook until golden in color:
1/2 cup olive oil
3 onions, sliced coarse
Add:
12 ounces fresh mushrooms,
chopped
4 bay leaves (discard)
2 tablespoons fresh oregano,
chopped
1 tablespoon fresh thyme,
chopped

1 tablespoon fresh basil,
chopped
1 teaspoon cumin seed, ground
1/2 teaspoon fresh ground
black pepper
4 vegetable cubes
Cook about 30 minutes, then add:
1 medium can steaklets, ground
(Note: Do not use burger, as
it has its own special flavor
which will not enhance this
mixture.)
1 tablespoon savita
1 cup water
Simmer for 3 hours. Do not
boil vigorously.

LIGHT TOMATO SAUCE

Bring to boil:
1 48-ounce can tomato juice
1 vegetable cube
1 bay leaf (discard after
heating)
1/2 teaspoon herb salt
1/2 teaspoon basil
1/2 teaspoon marjoram
This sauce is good to dip the
deep fried pimiento relleno in
and let it absorb some of the
tomato fragrance. The sauce
will keep several days if
refrigerated.

ITALIAN SPAGHETTI SAUCE

Cook until clear:
1/3 cup olive oil
2 cups onions, minced
4 cloves garlic, minced
Add and continue to cook
slowly:
1 No. 2-1/2 can tomatoes
(Italian style)
5 6-ounce cans tomato paste
2 ounces dry mushrooms
(soaked first) or
8 ounces fresh mushrooms
1 cup parsley, minced
1 tablespoon sugar
10 vegetable cubes
Pound in mortar and add:
1 teaspoon salt
1 teaspoon MSG (optional)
1 teaspoon basil
1 teaspoon rosemary
1 teaspoon thyme
1 teaspoon ground pepper
1 teaspoon cumin seed, ground
Simmer very gently for at least
2 hours, more if desired.
Vegetable balls may be put in
at the last and left soaking
for 1 hour. Do not cook or
balls may dissolve. Serve
over spaghetti.

sauces

SEED SAUCE FOR CARROTS

Put into blender and run for
2 minutes:
1 tablespoon celery seeds
1 tablespoon poppy seeds
1 tablespoon sesame seeds
1 teaspoon onion salt
1/4 teaspoon peppercorns
5 gratings fresh nutmeg
Melt in small saucepan:
3/4 pound butter
Add seed mixture to butter.
Spoon over small carrots that
have been steamed in pressure
cooker for 3 minutes at
15 pounds. Store in refrigerator—
will last one or two weeks.

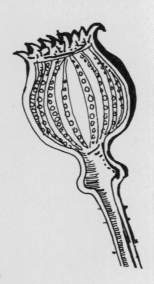

BUTTERMILK SAUCE FOR ASPARAGUS

Mix together and heat in
saucepan:
1 cup rich cream sauce (page 14)
1/3 cup buttermilk
1 teaspoon lemon juice
1/8 teaspoon herb salt
large pinch turmeric
dash cayenne
Cook until clear and add:
1 shallot or green onion,
including top, chopped fine
2 tablespoons butter
Thicken with:
1 tablespoon cornstarch,
dissolved in a little water
This sauce is also good on
broccoli and cauliflower.

SAUCE OLIVOS
for swiss chard, broccoli
or cauliflower.

Heat slowly in saucepan:
1/2 pound butter
2 tablespoons Bakon yeast
2 tablespoons capers, mashed
with a little of the juice
1/3 cup chopped ripe olives
Do not boil as this curdles
the sauce.

HOLLANDAISE SAUCE

(Quick and easy) Melt
in saucepan:
1/2 pound butter
Add and bring to boil:
1/4 cup lemon or lime juice
mixed in enough water
to make 2/3 cup
Heat blender top by rinsing
in hot water and
while it is hot add:
3 egg yolks (room temperature)
dash cayenne pepper
dash herb salt
dash chervil
When mixture in saucepan is
boiling, start blender and add
liquid immediately. Blend
for about 10 seconds, no more.
After sauce has set more
blending tends to thin it.
Keep warm in double boiler.

LOW CALORIE SAUCE FOR VEGETABLES

Heat in saucepan:
1 cup buttermilk
1/2 cup yogurt
Grind in mortar and add:
1 teaspoon ground lemon thyme
1 teaspoon herb salt
Then grind and add:
1 teaspoon capers
1/2 teaspoon turmeric
Dissolve in a little water and add:
1 tablespoon cornstarch
Cook until thickened, stirring constantly. Serve with broccoli or chard.

VARIATION ON LOW CALORIE SAUCE

Heat together until thick:
2 cups buttermilk
4 tablespoons yogurt
4 tablespoons cornstarch
Grind together, then add and heat again:
1/2 teaspoon herb salt
1/2 teaspoon winter savory
1-1/2 tablespoons capers
1 teaspoon turmeric

SAUCE FOR CROOKNECK YELLOW SQUASH

Heat but do not boil:
8 tablespoons butter
4 tablespoons lemon juice
Grind in mortar and add:
1/2 teaspoon herb salt
4 sprigs lemon thyme, or
1/4 teaspoon dry thyme
Put into blender to homogenize. Spoon over squash which has been steamed in pressure cooker for 3 minutes without pressure cap.

PIQUANT SAUCE FOR GREENS

Grind together:
1/2 teaspoon lemon thyme
1 teaspoon herb salt
Add:
1/2 teaspoon turmeric
Put herbs in saucepan along with:
4 ounces butter
juice of 1 lemon
Heat mixture, then thicken with:
1 teaspoon cornstarch, mixed in
1/2 cup water

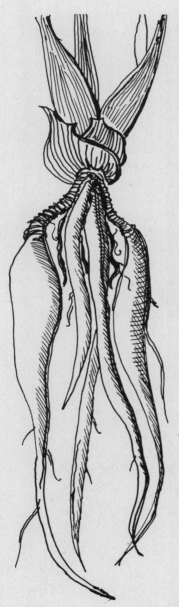

sauces

SWEET PEPPER BUTTER

Steam until soft then chop
fine:
1 green pepper
Cut into very small bits:
1 canned pimiento
Whip at room temperature until
light and fluffy:
2 sticks butter
Add:
1/2 teaspoon herb salt
Fold green pepper and pimiento
into butter.

GREEN ONION BUTTER

Cook in covered pan until
well done but not brown:
2 tablespoons butter
2 tablespoons onion, minced
Whirl in blender 1 minute:
the cooked onion
1/4 teaspoon MSG (optional)
3 green onion tops, chopped
2 tablespoons water
Whip until light and creamy:
**2 sticks butter (room
temperature)**
Add onion mixture and whip
until blended. This sauce is
excellent on baked, boiled
or mashed potatoes, also
on steamed rice.

GARLIC BUTTER

Cook until well done but
not brown:
3 cloves garlic, minced
2 teaspoons butter
Add, then whirl in blender
for 1 minute:
1 teaspoon garlic salt
1/2 teaspoon herb salt
Whip until light and fluffy:
4 ounces butter
Add garlic mixture and whip
until blended. This is
excellent on steamed zucchini.

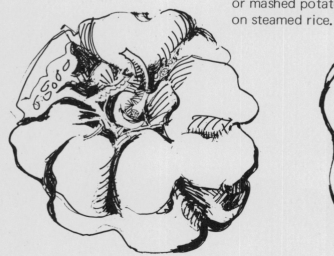

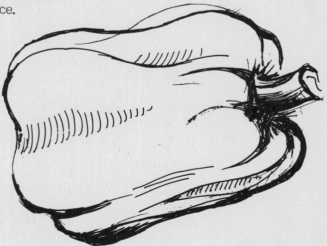

soups

SOUP—THE GOOD START

Because I am a self-taught cook, I have been able to embark on a journey of flavors not conditioned by the traditions of haute cuisine. Being a vegetarian, there were no stock pots to draw on. Herb seasonings are of the utmost importance in vegetarian cookery and these were the bulwark and foundation of my knowledge. When the basis of flavoring rests on beef, fowl and fish, the possibilities for variety in flavoring are altogether too limited. In all my experiments I have tried to branch out as much as possible, using the efficacy of fresh herbs. Such a variety of flavors is possible and thus the inventive spirit can begin to flower.

The dominant feature of a soup is the liquid and this liquid takes its character from one or a combination of vegetables. With the help of various herbs and spices the panorama of flavors is further extended. Some soups accumulate; others are always made from scratch. All juices from cooked vegetables should be faithfully saved and stored in the refrigerator; all scraps of vegetables that are still fresh should likewise be saved and stored in a plastic bag or humidifier. Some soups are served with no thickening at all; others need a little binding, the addition of various forms of roux. So, the chance to employ the full scope of one's imagination is almost unlimited.

Are you intrigued by now? I hope so, for in experimenting with this marvelous old menu stand-by, many of the secrets you learn will be found useful in all your other cooking.

soups

MINESTRONE

Soak overnight in 1 quart water:
1 cup garbanzo beans
Next day, cook beans 20 minutes at 15 pounds in
pressure cooker. Cook until done in 1 pint water:
2 small onions, chopped fine
2 stalks celery, chopped fine
1 small can tomatoes, mashed
2 zucchini, sliced thin
1 carrot, chopped fine
1/2 green pepper, chopped fine
1 bay leaf (discard after using)
1 pinch thyme, minced
1 pinch savory, minced
1/8 teaspoon marjoram, minced
1/8 teaspoon basil, minced
1/8 teaspoon rosemary, minced
Braise lightly:
2 garlic cloves, chopped
1 tablespoon olive oil
Dissolve:
12 vegetable cubes in
1-1/2 quarts water
Combine all ingredients, heat to boiling
and serve with plenty of
grated parmesan cheese
Serves 8.

FRESH TOMATO AND CORN SOUP

Wash, core but do not peel:
3 pounds tomatoes
Cook in pressure cooker for 2 minutes at 15 pounds pressure with:
1 pint water
Cut kernels from the cob without scoring them:
2 ears corn
Add to corn kernels and cook for 7 minutes:
2 tablespoons butter
1/2 cup water
1 bay leaf (discard after cooking)
1 pinch thyme leaves, rubbed to powder in palm of hand
1/4 teaspoon marjoram
1/4 teaspoon basil
1/2 teaspoon MSG (optional)
2 turns fresh pepper from pepper mill
5 vegetable cubes
Put cooked tomatoes through a sieve (or Foley mill if you have one), and add to the corn mixture when it is done. Return to stove to heat for 10 minutes to blend flavors before serving. Serves 6.

SPICED VEGETABLE AND TOMATO SOUP

So you want to cheat a little? OK . . . Purchase two cans of you know—the old standard, Campbell's tomato soup. This you will disguise so your family and friends won't know—perhaps. There will be as much or more work than if you had started from scratch.

Grind together in mortar or blender:
1/2 teaspoon corriander seed
1 cardamon seed (inside only)
1/4 teaspoon turmeric powder
1/8 teaspoon cumin seed powder
4 black peppercorns
1/8 teaspoon celery seeds
1/8 teaspoon poppy seeds
In a pan which can be tightly covered, fry the spice mixture **very slowly** for about 10 minutes with:
1 tablespoon butter
Add and steam until just tender, not mushy:
2 scallions, including tops, cut fine
1 small carrot, cut very fine
1/4 cup water
pinch of basil
1/2 cup celery, cut very fine
1/2 bay leaf (discard after cooking)
2 radishes, chopped fine
Now add and simmer for 10 minutes to blend flavors:
2 cans tomato soup!
2 cans water
You can now serve this as your own "makin's" and no one will know the difference—maybe. Garnish with finely chopped parsley. Serves 4.

SEVEN BEAN SOUP

What a marvelous soup this is—for it has nutritional value, excellent flavor and a good hearty body. Don't let the list of ingredients throw you off the track. Just plunge ahead and the final taste will be worth any extra trouble it takes to prepare. Some markets carry a package containing many varieties of beans—just enough for this recipe.
Soak overnight:
1/4 cup of each variety:
yellow split peas
green split peas
red kidney beans
small soup beans
garbanzos
lima beans
pinto beans
1-1/2 quarts water
Next day, cook beans in pressure cooker at 15 pounds for 20 minutes.

Mix together and cook until done but not mushy:
1 cup onions, chopped fine
1 cup green peppers, chopped fine
1/2 cup celery, chopped fine
1/2 cup carrots, chopped fine
1/2 cup parsley, chopped fine
1 clove garlic, chopped fine
2 tablespoons butter
1 quart plus 1 cup water
Mix beans and vegetables together and add:
2 bay leaves (discard when cooked)
1/4 teaspoon marjoram
1/4 teaspoon basil
1 pinch savory leaves
1 pinch thyme leaves
12 vegetable cubes
1 cup chopped ripe tomatoes
Simmer 20 minutes to blend flavors. No need to garnish this interesting soup. Serves 8.

soups

CREAM OF PIMIENTO SOUP

Cook in pressure cooker at
15 pounds pressure for
10 minutes:
3 large potatoes
peeled and cut in quarters
3/4 cup water
Drain and save liquid. Cook
until clear and tender,
but not brown:
1 large leek, cut fine, or
1 small onion, minced
1/2 cup water
2 teaspoons herb salt
1/4 teaspoon soup herb blend
2 vegetable cubes
Drain and save liquid. Heat
1 pint of the broth from
previously cooked vegetables
(adding more water if needed)
with:
2-1/2 pints milk
1/2 pint coffee cream
Combine all ingredients and put
through blender until smooth;
then add, stirring in well:
2 7-ounce cans diced pimientos
Heat to serving temperature.
Garnish with:
finely chopped parsley
Serves 6.

CREAM OF BROCCOLI SOUP

Cook for 2 minutes in pressure
cooker without the pressure cap:
1/2 cup water
2 heads broccoli
Drain, discard broth. Make a
roux with:
6 tablespoons butter
6 tablespoons flour
Add to roux and cook until
thick:
1 pint milk
1 pint coffee cream
1 bay leaf (discard when cooked)
Using half of the broccoli, whirl
cooked mixture in blender after
adding:
1-1/2 teaspoons herb salt
2 vegetable cubes
Chop the remainder of the
broccoli and add to soup. Heat
to serving temperature. Sliced,
stuffed olives can be used as a
garnish. Float them on top with
their little red eyes showing.
Serves 4.

SNOW-WHITE SOUP

Cut into 8 pieces, cook in
pressure cooker without cap for
2 minutes:
1 medium head of cauliflower
1/2 cup water
Drain and discard broth.
Make a roux with:
6 tablespoons butter
6 tablespoons flour
Add and cook until thick:
1 pint milk
**1 bay leaf (discard
when cooked)**
Put cooked mixture and half
of cauliflower in blender and
whirl until liquified, with:
1 pint coffee cream or milk
1-1/2 teaspoons herb salt
2 vegetable cubes
Reheat in double boiler,
adding the remainder of the
cauliflower which has been
finely chopped. (Half is
blended, half chopped, for
texture.) Garnish with plenty
of shredded sharp cheddar
cheese. This is a wonderful
soup for a starter at a formal
meal. The cheese is very
important. Serves 4.

CREAM OF WATERCRESS SOUP

If you have a stream running through your garden as we do here at the Ranch House, where watercress can grow along its banks, you are indeed lucky. Gather the watercress without taking the seed pods or flowers. (If less fortunate, you will have to use the 'store bought' variety.) Anyhow, here is a delicious soup:

Cook in pressure cooker at 15 pounds pressure for 10 minutes:
3 peeled potatoes, cut in thirds
1 cup water
Cook until clear:
1/2 cup chopped shallots or the white part of leeks
2 tablespoons butter
In blender, liquefy the potatoes and onions in:
1 quart milk, hot but not boiling

(Boiling liquid will blow out top of blender.) Strain potato mixture through sieve. Wash, chop off and reserve tops of:
1 bunch watercress

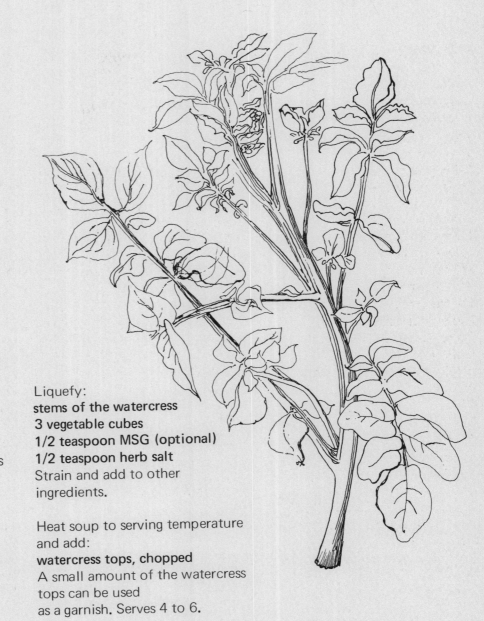

Liquefy:
stems of the watercress
3 vegetable cubes
1/2 teaspoon MSG (optional)
1/2 teaspoon herb salt
Strain and add to other ingredients.

Heat soup to serving temperature and add:
watercress tops, chopped
A small amount of the watercress tops can be used as a garnish. Serves 4 to 6.

soups

GAZPACHO

Making this soup is so easy it is almost a pity, for anything this good should be difficult and take a long time to make. But here it is in all its glory:

Put into blender and whirl for 1 minute:
1 No. 2-1/2 can tomatoes
1/2 teaspoon dry basil
1 pinch marjoram
1-1/2 teaspoons herb salt (very essential)
1/2 teaspoon lemon or lime juice
2 teaspoons silantro or coriander leaves (very essential)
Add and whirl 1/2 minute:
1/4 cup good imported olive oil
Strain, then add:
1/3 peeled cucumber
cut in very small cubes, seasoned with
sprinkling of herb salt
a small tomato, cubed and seasoned
1/2 green pepper, chopped fine
Refrigerate at least 24 hours then serve in cold bowls with garnish of finely chopped silantro or chives. Serves 4.

A guest at the Ranch House, just returned from South America, told us of another way of serving gazpacho—as a mid-day meal, very elaborately, with many chopped vegetables and other things. The soup is served in individual large, chilled bowls. The garnishes—anything that will go well with the soup's tomato flavor such as the cucumber, tomato and green pepper mentioned above; finely chopped green onions; sliced hard-boiled egg; green and ripe olives; finely sliced celery; almost any fresh vegetable—these are served in small bowls from which the diner makes his own selection.

CREAM OF PARSLEY SOUP

Put into blender and run until liquified—do it in 2 parts, it's easier:
1 quart whole milk
1 pint coffee cream
5 vegetable cubes
1/2 teaspoon soup herb blend
1/2 teaspoon herb salt
1 bunch fresh parsley, tops only

Heat in double boiler to serving temperature. Garnish with a sprinkling of paprika. Cubes of avocado may be added if desired. Serves 6.

This soup must not be heated too much as it tends to curdle. If it should curdle, return it to blender to smooth it out.

CREAM OF FRESH SPINACH SOUP

Boil for 3 minutes:
3 bunches fresh spinach
1 cup water
1/8 teaspoon summer savory (2 sprigs)
1/8 teaspoon marjoram (2 sprigs)
1/8 teaspoon thyme (2 sprigs)
2 leaves costmary or mint
1 tablespoon herb salt
5 vegetable cubes
2 turns pepper grinder
In blender liquify in:
1 quart milk
1 quart half and half (coffee cream)
Reheat but do not boil, then add:
2 tablespoons butter.
Serves 8.

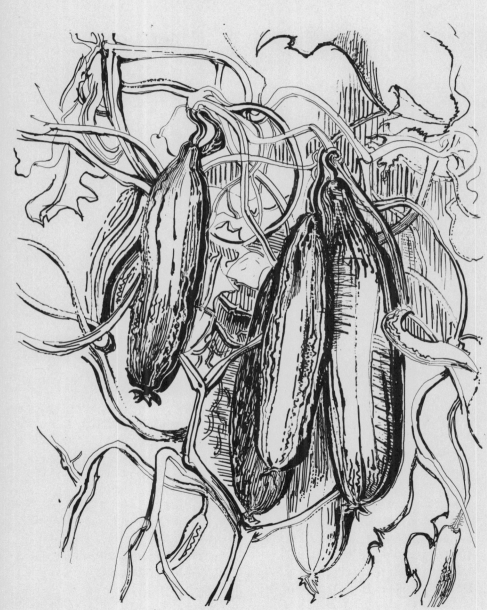

CHILLED CUCUMBER CREAM SOUP

Cook in pressure cooker at
15 pounds pressure for 3 minutes:
3 peeled and quartered cucumbers
1/2 cup green onions, no tops!
1 cup water
1/2 teaspoon chervil
1 teaspoon salt
1 tablespoon herb salt
good dash white pepper
Mix well together, add to
cooked cucumber mixture and
simmer gently for 2 minutes
to thicken:
2 tablespoons flour
1/4 cup water
Liquefy in blender and strain
into large pan. Mix together
and then liquefy in two parts:
1 cup coffee cream
1 peeled raw cucumber, halved
Strain this into large pan
containing the other ingredients,
then add:
1 pint whipping cream
Stir well together with wire
whip, then set aside to chill.
For best taste, chill overnight.
Serves 4.

soups

GREEN GODDESS SOUP

Cook until just done:
1 small bunch asparagus
1/4 cup water
Heat, but do not boil:
4 cups fresh green peas in
1/4 cup water
Liquefy the above and strain into:
1-1/2 quarts warm milk
To which has been added:
1/4 teaspoon marjoram (4 sprigs)
2 mint leaves
pinch thyme (1 sprig)
1-1/4 tablespoons herb salt
Liquefy without straining and
add to above:
1 large avocado in
1 pint milk
Heat and serve. Garnish with
unsweetened whipped cream and
parsley.

A good idea, when there is
fresh asparagus available, is to
save the bottoms of a couple of
bunches for this soup. The peas
are better and retain their fresh
flavor more if they are only
heated, not boiled. Of course
the soup cannot be boiled after
the avocados have been added,
because overheating creates a
strong acid flavor. This has
been an extremely popular soup
at the Ranch House and many
people have been unable to
identify the ingredients. It
should be light in color.
Serves 8.

GREEN BEAN BISQUE

Cook for 1 minute at 15 pounds
pressure:
4 cups fresh green beans
1/2 cup water
Liquefy with:
1 quart warm milk
1 tablespoon herb salt
pinch thyme (1 sprig)
1/8 teaspoon marjoram (2 sprigs)
1/8 teaspoon basil (1 leaf)
dash celery seed
dash freshly ground pepper
1 tablespoon sugar
Adjust seasoning with:
onion salt
Then add:
1/2 tablespoon sherry
Heat over water to serving
temperature but do not boil.
Serve with sliced almonds, well
toasted. If the almonds are
sliced very thin and toasted
well they will float on
the soup. Serves 6.

28

GREEN SPLIT PEA SOUP

Cook at 15 pounds pressure
15 minutes the following:
2-1/2 quarts hot water
1 pint green split peas
5 vegetable cubes
1/8 teaspoon fresh ground
black pepper
1/4 teaspoon MSG (optional)
1 teaspoon herb salt
1 teaspoon soup herbs
1 bay leaf (remove after cooking)
Cook for 2 minutes, without
pressure cap, then add to above:
1/2 green pepper, chopped fine
1/2 large carrot, chopped fine
1/2 cup celery, cut fine
1/2 large onion, chopped fine
1/2 cup hot water
Reheat for serving. Serves 8.

FRENCH ONION SOUP

A man I talked to in the office
of the French Consul in New
Orleans told me that true French
onion soup is made without meat.
The trick of getting the real
brown flavor, especially without
meat stock, is to simmer the
onions very, very slowly in
butter until they turn dark

brown. This develops the
delicious brown flavor and gives
the soup a body which it doesn't
otherwise have.

Slice as thin as possible:
6 large onions, the stronger
flavored, the better
Melt in a large frying pan:
3 tablespoons butter

Add half of the onions. Cover
and cook slowly until brown. If
cooked too fast, they will
scorch and the flavor will be
wrong. They must be cooked to a
mush when finished. Cook the
remainder of the onions in the
same way.

In large covered kettle put:
6 cups hot water
8 vegetable cubes, dissolved
8 fresh sorrel leaves, chopped
fine
Add browned onions and simmer
for at least 1 hour, on a very
low heat.

Serve with croutons and grated
Parmesan cheese. Croutons made
of dry French bread (preferably
sour dough) are best. Serves 8.

AVOCADO SOUP

For each serving, heat in
saucepan, but do not boil:
1 cup whole milk
1 teaspoon butter
1/8 teaspoon onion salt
dash of garlic salt
dash of MSG (optional)
Add:
1/2 avocado, very ripe, mashed,
but not too fine
Beat with rotary beater
constantly while heating soup,
until it is very hot. Serve with
dash of paprika, diced pimiento
or other garnish.

Avocado soup is wonderful if
you have lovely fresh, ripe
avocados on hand. It is a
simple soup, the main thing
being to have the milk very hot
but of course not boiling; then
add the other ingredients.
Whipping the soup as it heats
gives it a frothy texture which
is nice; and you have a chance
to use your own imagination
in garnishing it. Do not try to
keep it hot very long before
serving, as it will develop an
acid taste. Serves 1.

soups

FRENCH SORREL SOUP

We grow our own sorrel and can therefore serve a chilled sorrel soup just as it is made in France. We had grown sorrel for salads ever since we first had the restaurant up on the hill, but I had never heard of sorrel soup until someone exclaimed about our having fresh sorrel and said she had had a most delicious chilled sorrel soup in France. And so we now have it.

Helen and I were going on vacation, leaving the restaurant in charge of Marjorie Smith and a young fellow by the name of King Hutchinson. I suggested to him that he try to concoct a soup out of the sorrel we had growing. He had not done much cooking, but he seemed to have a flair for it, and did succeed in making the soup, so I cannot claim credit for the basic recipe, though I did refine it somewhat.

The main thing is to have enough fresh sorrel so that its tartness is imparted to the soup. The addition of carrots gives a bit of sweetness, and this can be adjusted if one does not care to have a very tart soup. Carrots will sweeten it without adding sugar.

We do the whole soup in a kettle and then put it through the blender and strain it. At first, when the soup has just been made, it may seem to lack flavor, but letting it stand 24 hours will bring out all the hidden flavor. It should be put into a covered stainless steel pot or glass vessel and kept overnight in the refrigerator. Sometimes people ask what kind of cheese we put in it, probably because of the combination of tartness and sour cream used as a garnish.

Cook in pressure cooker
10 minutes at 15 pounds:
7 cups water
1 large carrot, chopped fine
2 stalks celery, cut fine
1/2 small cucumber, chopped fine
1 medium onion, cut fine
2 large leaves cabbage, chopped
1/2 teaspoon soup herbs
5 vegetable cubes
1/4 cup parsley, chopped
Cook 5 minutes in separate pot, slowly:
6 large sorrel leaves and stems
1/4 cup water
Combine all ingredients and put through blender and strain. Then add:
1 tablespoon lemon juice
Chill 24 hours and serve with sour cream. Serves 8.

FRESH CORN BISQUE

Prepare:
3 ears fresh corn
by standing each ear on end and
with a sharp knife, cutting
each row of kernels down
the center, then scraping the
cob with the back of the knife
blade to get out all milk.
Combine corn with:
1/2 cup water
pinch thyme (1 sprig)
3/4 teaspoon herb salt
dash celery seed
dash fresh ground pepper
pinch marjoram (1 sprig)
1 pinch basil (1 leaf)
3 vegetable cubes
Cook 7 minutes, then liquefy
in blender with:
2 quarts hot milk
Strain, return to stove and add:
1/4 teaspoon MSG (optional)
1 tablespoon butter
1 tablespoon sugar

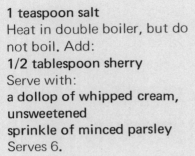

1 teaspoon salt
Heat in double boiler, but do
not boil. Add:
1/2 tablespoon sherry
Serve with:
**a dollop of whipped cream,
unsweetened
sprinkle of minced parsley**
Serves 6.

Of course, some corn is sweeter
than others, and the amount of
sugar used should be governed
by this. You may find that you
will have to double the amount
given in the recipe or use less,
if the corn is very fresh and
unusually sweet. Many times
the growers have allowed their
soil to become depleted and when
its minerals are exhausted corn
cannot manufacture its sugar.
Also, the sugar changes to
starch in about 4 hours, so most
corn from the market has already
gone through this stage.

soups

CREAM OF ONION SOUP

Cook in covered saucepan for
12 minutes:
1 tablespoon butter
2 cups sliced onions
1/4 green pepper, chopped
1/4 bunch parsley stems, minced
1/2 stalk celery, chopped fine
1/2 teaspoon soup herbs
1/2 teaspoon MSG (optional)
8 vegetable cubes
Heat and cook until slightly
thick:
2 quarts milk (1 pint cream
optional)
2 tablespoons cornstarch
Add onion mixture to thickened
milk and heat again over water,
being careful not to boil or heat
too much as this will cause it
to curdle.

Serve with croutons and a
sprinkle of grated cheese.
Serves 8.

LENTIL SOUP

Cook in pressure cooker
15 minutes at 15 pounds
pressure:
2 quarts water
1 pint tomato juice or stewed
tomatoes
1 small carrot, cut very fine
2 cups onions, minced
3 stalks celery, cut fine
1/2 green pepper, cut fine
1/2 cup parsley, chopped
1/2 cup cabbage, cut fine
3 bay leaves (discard)
1/4 teaspoon black pepper,
freshly ground
2 cloves garlic, minced
1/2 teaspoon MSG (optional)
1 tablespoon soup herbs
1/2 cup lentils, well washed
10 vegetable cubes
If you wish to make the soup
a main dish, use twice the
amount of lentils. This will
make a delicious, rich soup.
Serves 10.

BLACK BEAN SOUP

Soak overnight in warm water
set over pilot on stove:
1-1/2 pounds red kidney beans
2 quarts water
Cook at 15 pounds pressure
1 hour:
soaked beans
1 quart hot water
3 stalks celery, chopped fine
2 cups onion, chopped fine
1 green pepper, cut fine
1/4 teaspoon black pepper,
freshly ground
8 vegetable cubes
When cooked, put through
blender and while hot add:
1/2 teaspoon MSG
1/2 teaspoon herb salt
2 tablespoons fresh lime or
lemon juice
1-1/2 tablespoons sherry
Serve hot, garnished with
slices of lime or lemon and hard
cooked egg, minced. Serves 10.

CREAM OF FRESH GREEN PEA SOUP

Heat but do not boil:
4 cups fresh peas
1/2 cup water
Liquefy peas in blender with:
1-1/2 quarts milk at room temperature
1/4 teaspoon marjoram (4 sprigs)
pinch thyme (1 sprig)
2 mint leaves
1 tablespoons herb salt
1 tablespoon sugar
Put through sieve, then heat over water to serving temperature. Do not boil. Serves 8.

This is one of our most popular blender soups. The important thing in getting the flavor of this soup just right is in not cooking the peas. This also preserves their lovely green color. I tried having the milk hot and putting the peas in that way, but this caused the milk to froth so that it ran out over the top of the blender. You can avoid this mistake, since I have already made it for you.

CREAM OF POTATO SOUP

Cook in pressure cooker at 15 pounds pressure for 10 minutes:
4 large potatoes, peeled and cut in quarters
1 cup water
Cook until clear and done but not brown:
2 large leeks, cut fine, or
1 very large onion, minced
(leeks are best because of high sugar content)
1/2 cup water
1 tablespoon herb salt
1/2 teaspoon soup herb blend
1/2 teaspoon garlic salt
1/2 teaspoon MSG (optional)
Heat but do not boil:
2-1/2 quarts milk
1 pint coffee cream
Combine ingredients and put through blender, then heat to serving temperature in double boiler. When hot, add and stir in:
4 tablespoons butter
Serve immediately with:
croutons dusted with paprika
finely chopped parsley
Serves 6.

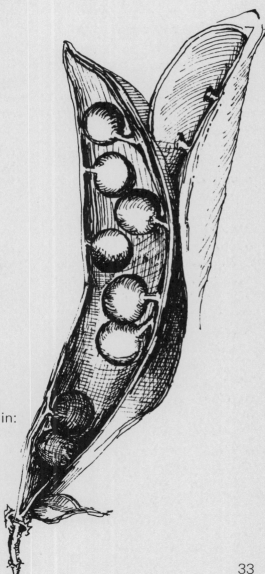

soups

VICHYSOISSE

Cook slowly to avoid browning:
2 tablespoons butter
4 large leeks, using only the white part, minced
1/2 cup onions, minced
Boil until tender but not mushy:
6 large unpeeled potatoes
Drain potatoes and cool them enough to peel. Crush with fork and mix with cooked leeks.
Then add:
1-1/2 quarts water
4 vegetable cubes, mashed in the water
1 teaspoon MSG (optional)
Boil gently for 10 minutes. Do not allow to stick to bottom of pot, as this will spoil the flavor. Put through Foley mill, then through blender, quickly. Don't overwork in blender, or it will be slimy. Chill overnight in refrigerator.
Next day, add and stir well:
1 pint half and half (coffee cream)
2-1/2 cups whipping cream
Blend thoroughly with whip. Season with a few dashes nutmeg, to taste.
Serve with finely chopped chives as garnish. Serves 10.

CREAM OF CELERY AND PIMIENTO SOUP

Braise:
1 tablespoon butter
1/2 onion, cut fine
2 cups celery, cut fine
1/2 clove garlic, minced
Grind in mortar:
1/2 teaspoon herb salt
1/2 teaspoon soup herbs
Add all ingredients to:
1-1/2 quarts whole milk
Thicken with:
3 tablespoons cornstarch
mixed in a little water.
Add:
5 vegetable cubes
dissolved in a little water
1 small can chopped pimientos
Heat over water but do not boil, and serve with suitable garnish. This soup curdles quickly if kept too warm. Serves 8.

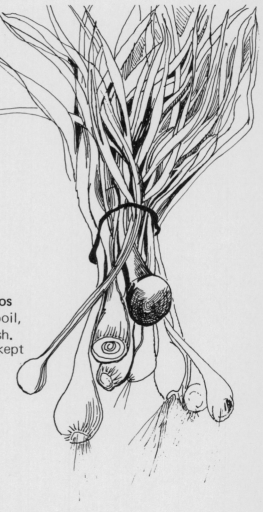

SOMETHING FROM RUSSIA

On a visit to New York, I stayed at the home of an old friend whose mother had come over from Russia, bringing many of the wonderful dishes of that country with her. While I was there she served chilled beet borsch, and of course I took her recipe for it and watched to see just how she made it. I usually omit the egg yolk from this recipe since I do not care for the flavor of uncooked egg yolk, but many people like it; it is a matter of individual taste. Some like chopped beets in this soup, others like to shred them to add texture. Still others like it clear, without any of the body of the beet. Also optional is whether or not the skins are left on the beets.

BEET BORSCH

Prepare by shredding with gricer, coarse cone, or grate on coarse grater; do not peel:
3-1/2 pounds beets
Cook in pressure cooker at 15 pounds for 15 minutes, with:

1-1/2 quarts water
1 large onion, chopped fine
1 tomato , or 1/2 can tomato sauce (Don't use too much)
juice of 1 large lemon, to taste
1 teaspoon salt
1 teaspoon sugar
1 teaspoon soup herbs
3 sorrel leaves (optional)
When cooked, put through Foley mill or strain. Use as much pulp as desired for thick or thin soup.
Add while hot, mixing with small amount of juice to keep from curdling:
1 egg yolk, lightly beaten (optional)
Should be piquant. Chill in refrigerator, preferably overnight.
Boil in pressure cooker at 15 pounds for 10 minutes, and cool immediately to reduce pressure:
4 unpeeled potatoes
Chop fine:
1 or 2 cucumbers
Add to each bowl of soup just before serving:
1/2 hot peeled potato
1 tablespoon chopped cucumber
1 large tablespoon sour cream
The potato must be very hot when dropped into the cold soup. Serves 8.

BEET AND CABBAGE BORSCH

Put through coarse cone of gricer and cook in pressure cooker for 10 minutes at 15 pounds:
1-1/2 pounds scrubbed and unpeeled beets
1 quart water
Liquefy in blender, adding
3 quarts more water.
Put into large pressure cooker and cook for 10 minutes at 15 pounds:
5 large stalks celery, cut fine
1-3/4 pounds cabbage, cut fine
4 ounces green peppers, cut fine
1 pound onions, cut fine
6 ounces carrots, cut fine
3 cloves garlic, chopped fine
1-1/2 teaspoons soup herbs
1-1/2 teaspoons salt
1/2 teaspoon MSG (optional)
10 vegetable cubes
1 ounce fresh lemon juice
1 quart water
Combine both mixtures in soup kettle and heat to serving temperature.
Serve with whipped sour cream and chopped parsley. Serves 10.

vegetables

VEGETABLES

"The kindly fruits of the earth."
—The Litany

ORGANIC GARDENING

With all of the chemicals injected into animals to be slaughtered for food and all the insecticide sprays used in large scale vegetable production, it is no wonder that more and more of us, in desperation, have decided to stop eating meat and to try raising our own vegetables, especially using the organic method.

If you're starting your own vegetable garden, bravo to you. The real hurdle is in beginning the project. Once it gets going, the rest is not too difficult and usually proves to be a happy experience. Your vegetables will not only be free of harmful chemicals, they will be more nutritious and taste better.

People tend to speak rather loosely about nature as being organic and inorganic. Probably they have in mind things that are visibly growing such as plant life (organic), and things that develop through a process like the formation of crystals (inorganic).

In organic gardening, various types of soil bacteria act to make the nutrients in the soil available to the plants. Inorganic minerals provide no food for this bacterial growth, so important in soil chemistry and soil rejuvenation. The breaking down of plant fibers releases their substances so that the bacterial action can take place. This process is easily accomplished by making a compost pile.

Set aside an area, about 5' by 5', for your compost pile. Collect grass clippings, leaves, weeds, anything that will decompose, enough to cover the area to a depth of about a foot when leveled off.

Now add a 3-inch deep layer of weed free manure. (Be sure it is weed free, not barnyard manure, or you will be pulling weeds all summer!) On top of the manure add a 3-inch layer of soil. When you have enough material for another layer, repeat this process. Now wet it down with a hose, and keep it moist, not wet. Make at least

four holes in the pile for ventilation. The pile is supposed to 'burn' not rot. To do this it needs moisture and oxygen. I've seen five-foot high piles with steam rising from the top of them.

When the pile is six weeks old turn it completely over. Don't bother about keeping it in layered order. Keep it moist— do not flood it, just moisten it thoroughly. Again make four or five holes with a pole or iron bar. In another six weeks it should be turning black. Wonderful light-textured soil is made this way, the kind that nature usually takes years to make.

When you begin to make your garden don't spread this wonderful compost soil all over it. Dig a trench for the row you are going to plant and put the enriched soil in it, then put the seeds directly on this soil. Cover them with the earth from the trench. After you have completed the planting, put chicken manure **between** the rows. It is very strong and the

vegetables

leaching from it will feed the roots of your plants. You will be amazed at the results from this method of gardening. Some gardeners find that keeping the soil around the plants moist discourages ants that put aphids at the tip of new growth. This avoids the necessity for spraying. If you plant early in the spring and the weather is cold, make — or buy from your nursery — small cone-shaped paper caps to put over each

plant. This will speed the growth. ***Don't let weeds get a start.*** They are easy to deal with when small, and pulling out large weeds disturbs the roots of the vegetables.

Eastern and midwestern gardeners should find out about making cold frames for midwinter and early spring gardening. This will extend the growing season and is worth the extra effort.

Select simple things that grow easily. In temperate climates Swiss chard, both red and green, grows wonderfully with little attention. Zucchini and yellow crookneck squash, eggplant and green peppers just grow like Topsy. Cabbage, red and green, is a fall crop. Radishes grow in six weeks, very easily.

Tomato plants are always great— watching those little blossoms turn into big red fruit is happiness. Don't plant them however, unless you arrange some way to keep the vines up so that the fruit will not be lying on the ground where insects, chewing bugs and rot can attack

it. The vines can be tied to poles. Four vines will produce more than enough fruit for the average family if properly tended, fertilized and watered. English peas, pole beans, scarlet runner beans take poles and tying up also. Cauliflower, broccoli and brussel sprouts are all buds of the flower plant and have to be picked before they open and go to seed. Celery must be grown in a moist environment or it develops a bitter taste. Root crops— turnips, carrots, beets, rutabagas, parsnips and, if you have the space, potatoes, should be planted according to instructions on the seed packages. Edible pod peas, called Grey's sugar peas on some packages (the kind that are served in Chinese restaurants) grow very easily as a winter crop in moderate climates. With these vegetables and a small herb garden as suggested elsewhere in this book, you're all set for a wonderful year of taste enjoyment. There's nothing like being able to go out and pick things from your own garden.

PREPARATION OF VEGETABLES

As soon as vegetables are picked they start turning their sugar to starch for storage purposes, so it can be utilized by the germ in the seed for the necessary nourishment when sprouting for new growth. Yes, the vegetable likes to perpetuate itself just as humans do. So, the sooner you get the vegetable onto the table after it is picked the more rich sugar flavor you will have. Remember the farmer's old saying about cooking sweet corn: "Put the water on the stove, and when it is about to boil go out and pick the corn."

Authorities say vegetables more than 24 hours old, not refrigerated or preserved in some manner, have lost 90 per cent of their nutritional value and much of their flavor. Here at the Ranch House people often remark about the wonderful flavor of the vegetables. There is no special magic in our methods, except that we make certain that the vegetables we use are fresh and we do not overcook them. If the cooking time is short the natural sugar content is not all lost, does not bleed out into the water or get driven off in the steam along with the volatile oils. For this reason we suggest pressure cooking. Also, nutritionists say the worst enemy of vitamins is heat in the presence of oxygen. The pressure cooker eliminates this for the air is dispersed by the steam before the cap is put on. Oxygen in the air "burns" all the vitamin A, and will turn freshly cut peaches brown. The quickness of the pressure cooking preserves the color of the vegetable, too. Then we serve them with a sauce that does not cover up the flavor but only enhances it.

We often use the pressure cooker for vegetables without using the cap. Even without the cap there is more pressure than there would be in a kettle with the closest fitting lid. Some vegetables take only a half minute in the pressure cooker so we use a timer to avoid overcooking. When the pressure cap is used the kettle has to be cooled immediately to reduce the pressure and prevent overcooking.

Here are some of the terms used in explaining how to prepare vegetables for cooking. We use four degrees of thickness in chopping:

Minced—Chopped very fine, almost to a mush

Fine—Sliced paper thin one way, and once across the other way

Chopped—Cut about 1/8 inch thick

Coarse—Cut about 1/2 inch thick

These degrees are important for the sake of both texture and flavor. If a sauce is to be made, in which only the flavor is needed, the vegetable is minced, If a slight texture is wanted, the vegetable is chopped fine; if texture is important but is still subsidiary to other ingredients, then "chopped" is used. In vegetarian cooking, when both flavor and texture are primary, the vegetable is cut coarse.

vegetables

ZUCCHINI

Zucchini should be picked when they are not more than 4 inches long. This way, the seed pods have not yet developed and the squash still retains its sweetness. Slice the zucchini exactly in half lengthwise. Season liberally with garlic salt (not the powder), and lay cut side up on a trivet in the pressure cooker, with 1/4 cup of water. A second layer crosses the first, making squares between. Cook only four minutes without the pressure cap, and when through steaming, lift the lid. Remove the halves without breaking them and serve cut side up, adding only a little soft butter.

CARROTS

Carrots should be very tiny, long and thin, no bigger around than your finger. If larger ones are used, they should be sliced thin diagonally. In cooking, use very little water and keep what is left. It makes a delicious addition to sauces and soups. Small carrots should not be peeled or skinned, for doing so lets out the flavor and natural sweetness. Cook them 3 minutes at 15 pounds pressure. At the end of this time, cool the pot immediately under running water. Lift and invert the lid. Serve whole, with a sauce spooned over them.

BEETS

The vegetable that suffers least from being canned is beets. They come in many ways and are so easily prepared, canned or fresh. When cooking fresh beet roots, do not skin them. Scrub them clean and put them through a gricer (See page 180). Use very little water and cook them for 10 minutes at 15 pounds pressure. If they are young enough only butter, pepper and salt need be added. There are fancier ways of serving beets but one treat not known to many people is to take the well-washed tops, if they are fresh and not wilted, and put them whole into the pot with only a little water and cook them quickly, then serve them with a sprinkling of herb salt and good sweet butter. Usually only those who have lived in the country have had this rare treat. Another rare treat is to take the new little beet tops and roots only about the size of peas which are taken out of the ground in the process of thinning out the rows of growing beets, wash them thoroughly and cook them quickly, then serve buttered and salted.

LIMA BEANS

Frozen Fordhook limas are excellent with the addition of fresh or dried thyme and herb salt. Use the usual 1/4 cup of water, no trivet, and cook them only 1/2 minute without the pressure cap. When the pot stops steaming, add plenty of butter and serve. Small cooked onions and limas make a wonderful combination.

CAULIFLOWER

Cauliflower can be such a good vegetable if it is not overcooked! It is also often served raw, the small buds added to vegetable salads. Since it is tasty without cooking, do not be afraid to leave it firm when you cook it.

Turn the cauliflower head upside down and make 4 to 6 cuts down through the stem, depending on the size of the head. Split the head apart, and break off small pieces, leaving a piece of stem on each bud. Put the pieces in the pressure cooker on a trivet and use 1/4 cup of water. Cook for only 1-1/2 minutes, without the pressure cap. When done, remove lid immediately, and when it stops steaming, invert the lid. Lay on plate in small clusters and add sauce.

GREEN CABBAGE

Green Cabbage is good cut into 1/2-inch squares and cooked quickly until just done but still crisp. Add poppy seeds and herb salt. Use very little water, so that when it is done there is practically none left. Add sliced pitted green-ripe olives, butter, and cream, not milk. Toss to incorporate all ingredients. Reheat, but do not boil. Each portion should be served in a small dish, without thickening the cream.

GREEN BUSH SQUASH

Green Bush Squash—the little flat round ones with slightly scalloped edges—should be cut into 6 or 8 pieces, like cutting a pie. Use a trivet in a saucepan, with a small amount of water. Season with dill seeds, a sprinkling of turmeric, butter, and herb salt. Be watchful in the cooking, as one moment it will seem not to be done and seconds later it will be mushy.

BROCCOLI

Broccoli is difficult to cook
without losing the natural
green color. It can be done,
however. Split the larger stalks
into 2 or 4 pieces, down
through the center. Lay them in
the cooker on a trivet, cut
side up. Use 1/4 cup water and
cook only 1/2 minute with the
cap, at 15 pounds pressure.
When done, hold the cooker
under a stream of cold water
until the pressure is normal.
Then lift and invert the lid.
Serve cut side down, with a
sauce spooned over it.

SWISS CHARD

Swiss Chard, red or green, is
often served at the Ranch House.
We use part of the white stem
for texture. The long leaves
with the stems attached are
laid on the chopping board
with the joint of the stems
and leaves together. Thus all
the stems can be cut off at
once and kept separate. The
leaves are shredded coarsely,
about an inch wide, and cut

crosswise; the stems are
chopped about 1/4 inch wide.
The chopped stems are put in
the bottom of the pot, with
just enough water to cover
them. The leafy part is then
laid on and they are cooked
1-1/2 minutes without the
pressure cap. When the pot
stops steaming, lift and invert
the lid. In serving, use equal
parts of the stems and leaves.
If only the leaves are cooked,
they tend to settle down and
become soggy.

CELERY

Celery, when used as a cooked
vegetable, must be left firm
and crisp. Cut the stalks into
1-inch pieces and season with
herb salt to taste. Cook 2
minutes without pressure cap.
When finished steaming, invert
the lid. For seasoning and
color, plenty of butter, herb
salt and chopped pimientos may
be added. Celery is also good
added to lima beans. Use 2 parts
celery, 1 part limas, cooked
separately and mixed together
with butter and pimiento.

GREEN STRING BEANS

Green String Beans have a
very strong taste. If they are
overcooked, this strong flavor
increases until they become
almost inedible.
String beans may be prepared in
any one of three ways—left
whole, French cut (that is,
split down the center
lengthwise), or cut across into
1-inch lengths. The French cut
is quickest cooked, the 1-inch
cut next, and the whole takes
the longest. Here are the
cooking times:
French Cut—1-1/2 minutes with
cap, then cool quickly
1-Inch—2 minutes with cap,
cool quickly
Whole—2-1/2 minutes with cap,
then break pressure
In European markets, a bouquet
garni of a small bunch of
summer savory and parsley is
always given with the purchase
of string beans. Herb salt
should be used generously,
they require plenty; also,
a liberal amount of butter when
serving. Onions, sliced very
thin, may be put on top of
the beans when cooking.

43

vegetables

JERUSALEM ARTICHOKES

Long before Europeans landed on this continent the natives were cultivating these tubers as one of their staple foods. How the name Jerusalem became attached to this member of the artichoke family is not clear—Webster suggests it may be a corruption of "girasole," the Italian word for sunflower. They are easy to raise—just plant the tubers in rows about six inches apart in well-drained soil. No need to cultivate them, and they will stand prolonged drought and neglect. A perfect plant for our leisure loving gardener of today. Frost does not hurt them and they are best left in the ground if they are not to be used immediately, for these thin-skinned tubers do not last very well after digging. They will keep for a few months refrigerated, however, if you have the storage space for them.

BUTTERED JERUSALEM ARTICHOKES

There are numerous ways to serve Jerusalem artichokes—au gratin, in a souffle, raw in salads, mixed with other vegetables, made into a cream soup, etc. One of the simplest ways, and one of the tastiest, is to butter-steam them: Put about
1/4 cup water,
4 tablespoons butter and
2-1/2 teaspoons salt
in a saucepan that can be covered tightly. (A pressure cooker used without the cap is excellent). Wash well
1 pound of Jerusalem artichokes
but do not peel, as much of the flavor is just under the skin. Slice about 1/4 inch thick and add to the pan and cook about 4 minutes. They should be done but still crisp. Shake them about instead of stirring so as not to break them up too much. No water should be left when they have finished cooking.

ASPARAGUS

When cooking asparagus, select tall, thick stalks. Wash well, being sure the little growing "flaps" on the sides of the stalks are clean. Hold the root end in one hand and with the other hand bend the stalk down; where it breaks is the line between the tough and the edible parts of the asparagus. Tie the stalks lightly in bunches, stand these bunches in 2 inches of water and boil until they can be pricked easily with a fork. The tenderer top part will be cooked by the steam and the tougher part by being immersed in the water. Remove the bunches, lay them down and cut the strings. Each stalk should be green and tender but not mushy. Salt lightly and add sauce or just melted butter.

BAKED ASPARAGUS AND PEAS

Cut into 1-inch pieces and boil until tender:
fresh asparagus, about 1 pound
Drain excess water.
Mix together for sauce:
2 tablespoons butter
2 tablespoons flour
Add and cook only until it begins to thicken:
2 cups milk (or half and half)
1/2 teaspoon herb salt
Add asparagus to the sauce.
Then add:
1 pound green peas
The peas should not be cooked. The sauce will cook them in the oven.

Grease a flat shallow baking pan and turn vegetables into it.
Sprinkle with:
dry bread crumbs
grated cheddar cheese (mild variety)—not too much
Dot with butter and bake only enough to make sauce bubble. Peas will then be done and top will be brown and crusty.

FRENCH PEAS

Bring to good boil, in sufficient water to prevent sticking:
2 cups peas
Shred into 1/2 inch widths:
1/2 cup head lettuce (The greenest part of head.)
Grind in mortar:
1/2 teaspoon onion salt
pinch garlic salt
pinch MSG (optional)
1/6 teaspoon ground marjoram
or 1/4 teaspoon marjoram leaves
pinch sugar (optional)
Add lettuce and herb mixture to nearly cooked peas and continue until just done but still firm.

Add:
2 tablespoons butter
Toss lightly and serve immediately.

vegetables

GREAN BEANS CALIFORNIAN

Saute in pressure cooker, without lid:
1 large onion, medium cut
Place over onions:
1 quart cut green beans
Add:
1/2 cup water
Grind in mortar and add:
1 teaspoon herb salt
6 sorrel leaves
2 costmary leaves
6 sprigs lemon thyme
1 sprig oregano
1 sprig summer savory
1 sprig marjoram
Cook for 1-1/2 minutes at 15 pounds pressure.

GREEN BEANS AND CAULIFLOWER

Cook in pressure cooker at 15 pounds pressure for 1-1/2 minutes then cool and drain:
1 quart cut up green beans
1/4 cup water
Cook in pressure cooker without cap, until just done but firm (about 2 minutes):
1 head cauliflower, broken into buds, not too fine
1/2 teaspoon poppy seeds
1/4 cup water
Make a roux with:
4 tablespoons butter
2 tablespoons flour
1-1/2 teaspoons herb salt
Add and cook until thickened:
2-1/2 cups coffee cream
Combine vegetables, add sauce and stir gently. Heat in double boiler. Serve with toasted bread crumbs or toasted fried sliced almonds that have been lightly salted with herb salt.

GREEN BEANS HUNGARIAN

For a different vegetable that has the taste of eastern Europe, try this:

Wash and french-cut:
1-1/2 quarts green beans
Cook beans in pressure cooker without cap for about 3 minutes with:
1 onion sliced thin
1/2 teaspoon savory herb blend
1 teaspoon herb salt
Drain off excess water then add and stir in well without breaking up beans:
1/2 cup sour cream, whipped
Keep beans hot until serving time, then sprinkle with bread crumbs that have been browned slightly in butter and paprika. There won't be leftovers if you've followed this recipe!

GREEN BEANS WITH SUNFLOWER SEEDS

Wonderful textures and flavors are available in seed and nut meats and should not be overlooked in cooking.
This recipe is simple but the results are quite extraordinary. The thin, pencil-type green beans are not always available at the supermarket but they are best for this recipe.

Put in pressure cooker:
1 pound French-cut green beans
1/2 cup water
Scatter on top of beans:
1 large onion, sliced thin
Grind together and sprinkle over beans:
1/2 teaspoon savory herb blend
1 teaspoon herb salt
Now scatter over this:
1/4 cup hulled sunflower seeds

Cook without pressure cap until done to your taste — about 4 minutes. Drain off water and add:
1/2 stick of butter, sliced thin
Shake pot with rotary motion to mix butter into ingredients without breaking beans. Chop:
2 pimientos
and add them as a garnish before serving. This is the final touch to a delicious dish.

47

vegetables

ORANGE BEETS

Drain, retaining half of juice:
2 large cans beets
Add to beet juice:
1/4 cup orange juice
1/4 cup honey
2 tablespoons vinegar
1 tablespoon grated orange rind
1 ounce white Karo syrup
1/6 teaspoon powdered
cardamon seed
Thicken over heat with:
2 tablespoons cornstarch
dissolved in cold water
Pour thickened juice over
drained beets and add:
2 tablespoons butter
Heat over water so they will not
burn, and let stand to marinate
for at least 4 hours. Serves 8.

BEETS PIQUANT

Cut off tops leaving about
1 inch of stems, scrub but
do not peel:
1-1/2 pounds beets (about 10)
Put beets through gricer,
coarse cone, making them into
shoestring size. Put them in
pressure cooker with:
1/2 cup water
Grate rind of two oranges, then
cut oranges in half and juice
and add to beets:
juice of 2 oranges
gratings from 1 orange
Place on top of beets: (Open
side down, like 4 little hats)
4 halves of orange skins left
from juicing and grating
Spoon over orange hats:
1/4 cup honey
Cook 10 minutes at 15 pounds
pressure.
Remove orange skins and put
aside.

Add to beets:
1/2 teaspoon MSG (optional)
1/2 teaspoon herb salt
2 tablespoons melted butter
juice of 1/2 lemon
1/2 teaspoon powdered cardamon
seed
1 tablespoon cornstarch dissolved
in a little water
Reheat beets until sauce is
thickened, and serve.
Cut orange skins into pie-
shaped pieces, about 12 to each
half, and lay in pie pan, grated
side up. Spoon over pieces:
1/4 cup honey
Sprinkle with:
cinnamon
Reheat and serve on separate
dish as relish.

BAKED ONIONS

Peel and cut in half enough onions to pack the bottom of a buttered glass casserole that has a tight cover. Sprinkle onions with herb salt or with plain salt and a dash of black pepper. Cover the onions with fresh milk. Put on cover and bake at 325° for about 1-1/2 hours. The milk will evaporate and thicken and a wonderful sweetness will develop because of the concentrated onion and milk flavors.

BAKED ONIONS, CELERY AND CARROTS WITH CHEESE

Cook separately until just done, equal portions of:
very small onions
celery, cut in 1-inch lengths
carrots, cut in 1/2-inch lengths
Drain vegetables and add them to:
rich cream sauce (see sauces)
Turn mixture into well-buttered casserole and stick down into mixture:
1/2-inch lengths of sharp cheddar cheese wedges.
Adding the cheese in this manner keeps it from blending into the mixture. The taste of the cheese will retain its character, complementing the vegetable mixture. Bake at 350° until the top begins to brown and the cheese melts.

BAKED ONIONS WITH CHEESE

Peel and cut in half:
good, firm onions
Place in pan with cut side up and sprinkle with:
basil leaves rubbed to powder in palm of hand
herb salt
bread crumbs
Parmesan cheese
Bake for 15 to 20 minutes at 350°, until tender. Serve garnished with a strip of pimiento.

49

vegetables

SAUERKRAUT

Melt in frying pan:
**2 tablespoons butter or
margarine**
2 tablespoons Bakon yeast
Add:
1 large can kraut, drained
1/2 onion, minced
Cover and steam 30 minutes.

TOMATOES PORTUGESE

Cut rounds from slices of bread
and brown lightly in butter.
Cut thick rounds of tomato and
fry in butter. Add grated Swiss
cheese to rich cream sauce (see
sauces), enough to cover
tomatoes. Put tomato slices on
rounds of bread, pour sauce
over them and sprinkle with
more grated cheese. Brown
lightly under broiler and serve
immediately.

BROILED TOMATOES

Remove core, slice off top,
and put in shallow pan:
6 tomatoes
Mix together:
2 tablespoons butter
1/2 onion, minced very fine
2 stalks celery, minced fine
**2 tablespoons chives,
minced fine**
1/2 teaspoon savory herbs
1/2 teaspoon garlic salt
Season tomatoes lightly with
herb salt, add garnish mixture
and broil until tomatoes are
soft to touch. Sprinkle with
grated Romano cheese, return
to broiler and brown lightly.

EASY BROILED TOMATOES

Remove core and slice tomatoes
in 3/4-inch slices. Lay in
baking pan and sprinkle with
herb salt, then with powdered
basil, then with bread crumbs,
and lastly with grated
Parmesan or Romano cheese. Bake
until tomatoes are just soft.

TOMATOES AND
FRESH OKRA

Cook slowly in saucepan until
done, about 1 minute:
2 cloves garlic, minced
2 tablespoons olive oil
Wash and stem, without cutting
into seedpods:
1 pound fresh okra
Add okra to garlic and olive
oil, add
2 tablespoons water
cover and cook slowly until
tender—about 15 minutes.
Core and cut into quarters;
add to okra:
1 pound fresh tomatoes
Grind together and add:
1 teaspoon tomato herb blend
1 teaspoon herb salt
Cover tightly and bring just to
a boil; do not overcook the
tomatoes. When done add:
2 tablespoons butter
and let stand for 10 minutes
to blend flavors before
serving.

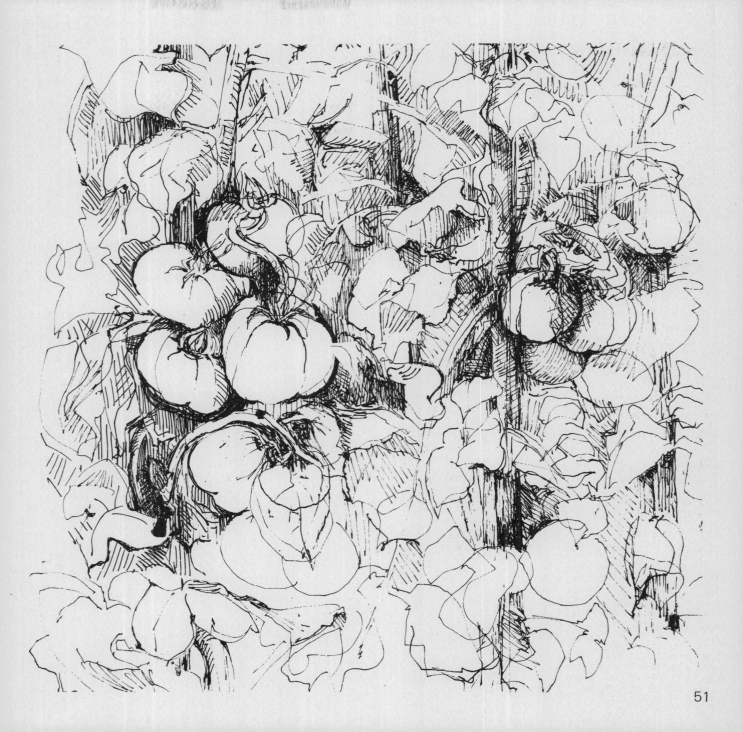

51

vegetables

CARROTS AND PINEAPPLE

Cook until just tender but not too soft:
2 large bunches large carrots, cut diagonally 1/2 inch thick
1/2 teaspoon herb salt
1/2 cup water
Cook together in saucepan:
1 14-ounce can crushed pineapple and juice
1-1/2 cups pineapple juice (unsweetened)
1-1/2 teaspoons cardamon seed, powdered
1 teaspoon poppy seeds
1/2 teaspoon herb salt
1/2 cup brown sugar
1 tablespoon cornstarch, dissolved in a little water
Add, and stir in well:
4 tablespoons butter
Combine the carrots and pineapple sauce in layers so that the carrots will not be broken up by stirring, and heat over water to prevent scorching.

CARROTS WITH SHERRY

This recipe is much too simple to taste that good!
Melt in an electric frypan:
1 stick butter (preferably sweet)
Wash, peel and slice thin:
carrots enough to cover bottom of pan about one inch deep.
Add no water! Cover, set temperature at 250° and allow plenty of time for the cooking. This will depend on the temperature of the carrots and their youngness; cook them until they are very soft and tender. This will take a long time. When they are done to your taste add:
2 ounces of sweet sherry.
Recover and cook until sherry saturates the carrots through and through. (A regular frypan can be used if the heat is kept down low.)

BROCCOLI IN CHEESE SAUCE

To make sauce, heat:
1 pint milk (do not boil)
Stir into milk a paste made
with a little warm water
mixed into:
1/4 cup flour
Mix together, heat and add to
sauce:
2 tablespoons butter
1 tablespoon Bakon yeast
1/2 teaspoon herb salt
Cook until thick over low flame,
stirring constantly.

Cook in salted water and drain:
1 pound fresh broccoli,
cut coarse
Cut into 1/2-inch squares and
add to broccoli
1/2 pound sharp cheddar cheese
Fold in sauce, put into
casserole and bake at 350°
for 30 minutes.

vegetables

CREAMED POTATOES HAROLDO

Cook until done:
4 large unpeeled potatoes
Peel potatoes, cut into
1/2-inch squares, and add:
1/2 teaspoon herb salt
1 teaspoon regular salt
Blend together and heat:
4 tablespoons butter
4 tablespoons flour
1/2 teaspoon herb salt
Add and bring to boil, then
combine with potatoes:
1-1/2 cups milk
1-1/2 cups half and half cream
Braise lightly in butter:
4 green onions, cut in
1/4-inch lengths
3/4 tablespoons parsley,
chopped fine
Garnish potatoes with onions
and parsley. Cheese may be
sprinkled on top and browned
under broiler.

BACK COUNTRY POTATOES AND TURNIPS

Peel equal portions of:
potatoes
white turnips
Slice very thin and let stand in
cold water for about an hour.
Put into skillet and heat until
little rivers begin to run in it:
peanut oil
enough to fry potatoes
and turnips
Drain potatoes and turnips and
put them in the hot oil,
laying them flat. Cover tightly
and cook slowly so that the
steam will cook them and they
will brown on the bottom. When
they are brown on one side,
turn them to brown on the
other side. Salt and pepper can
be added now or when they were
first put into the pan. They
should be brown and soft when
done. Another method is to cook
and mash the potatoes and
turnips together and then add
plenty of butter. This gives a
different taste and texture.

FLUFFY POTATO PANCAKES

Prepare:
1-1/2 cups raw grated potato
Beat until stiff but not dry:
3 egg whites
3/4 teaspoon salt
Beat until stiff :
and lemon colored
3 egg yolks
3/4 teaspoon salt
With wire whisk, thoroughly
but gently fold yolks into
beaten whites, and sift in:
3 tablespoons flour
1/6 teaspoon black pepper,
freshly ground
Gently fold in the raw
potatoes and add:
3 tablespoons onion,
minced very fine
Heat 1/4-inch of peanut oil
in deep griddle or frying pan.
Drop batter into oil, using
large cooking spoon. Baste the
cakes as they fry so they will
not come apart when turned.
Turn with pancake turner aided
with a spoon.

LOUISIANA
SWEET POTATOES

For a time I lived in the
French Quarter in New Orleans,
in the studio of my friend,
Audye Reynolds Tuttle, who now
lives here in Ojai. Her cook
had a marvelous way of
concocting a dish of sweet
potatoes. The recipe was Audye's
own and when she moved to Ojai
she gave it to me. Jersey
sweets, which are not the same
as yams, are not suitable for
this recipe. The yummiest yams
you can find are the best to
use.

Scrub and grate:
6 medium sized yams—
the kind with the dark,
purplish skins are best.
Add and mix well with the
grated yams:
1 cup milk
1 teaspoon nutmeg
1 teaspoon allspice
1/2 teaspoon cardamon
2 eggs
1 cup brown sugar

Spread mixture in greased glass
baking dish. Pour over it evenly:
1/4 pound melted butter
Bake at 400° for 30 minutes.
Insert knife to test.
Before serving, dot with:
**small marshmallows, (or cut large
ones), melted under broiler
whole pecan meats (optional)**
pressed into mixture are also
excellent.

YAMS WITH
FRESH ORANGE SAUCE

Cook until tender, then skin
and slice:
6 medium sized yams
Combine in pan and cook until
thickened:
1 cup orange juice
1 tablespoon cornstarch
3 tablespoons melted butter
1/3 cup brown sugar, packed
1/3 cup white sugar
rind of 1/2 orange, grated
2 tablespoons white corn syrup
Arrange yam slices in greased
baking dish. Pour sauce over
them and bake 45 minutes at 350°.

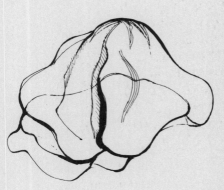

vegetables

BAKED SOY BEANS

Soak in water overnight:
1/2 pound soy beans
(Let stand over pilot light if
you have a gas stove.)
Pour off soaking water and add:
1 quart water
1 teaspoon salt
Cook in pressure cooker 45
minutes at 15 pounds pressure.
Do not undercook; they should
be soft and tender.
Braise until golden in color:
4 tablespoons butter
1 clove garlic, chopped fine
1 large onion, chopped—1-1/2 cups
1/2 cup celery, chopped fine
1/2 cup parsley, chopped fine
1/2 teaspoon summer savory
1/4 teaspoon MSG (optional)
Add to cooked beans, stirring
well. Place in baking dish and
bake slowly until water is gone,
but do not allow beans to dry.
Cover at end of baking so beans
will not dry on top. This is a
high protein dish and should
always be served accompanied
by a green vegetable and a
salad. Beans are a hearty dish
and are difficult for some
people to digest without the
aid of roughage.
56

ZUCCHINI TORRE

Cut into 1-inch thick slices,
lengthwise:
1-1/2 pounds zucchini
Fry on both sides in peanut oil
heated to 450°, until
tender and almost transparent.
(Peanut oil is essential,
because zucchini must be cooked
at high temperature.)
Grind in mortar:
3 culantro leaves
3 chilis
1 sprig rosemary
4 cloves garlic
1 teaspoon salt
Add to herbs:
1 6-ounce can tomato paste
1 No. 303 can peeled tomatoes
(small can)
Cook 5 minutes, stirring
constantly. Remove from flame.
Line bottom of a 12" x 15"
earthenware casserole with the
cooked zucchini. Spread on a
layer of the sauce.
Add a layer of:
aged cheddar cheese, sliced
rather thick
Cover with aluminum foil and
bake 45 minutes at 400°.

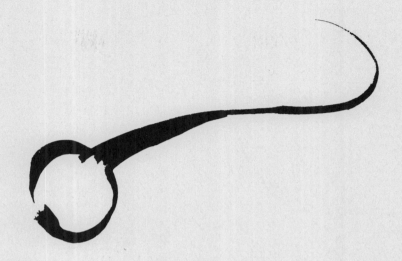

SALAD SUGGESTIONS

After experimenting with as many as ten varieties of lettuce in our Ranch House garden we have settled on a few favorites, selected for characteristics of flavor, texture and color. The bronze types are wonderful for color, and what can equal the Boston butter and the Bibb lettuce for taste and texture? The Kentucky Bibb lettuce may be called Limestone on a restaurant menu.

It is most important that the lettuce be fresh and very crisp and dry when used in salads. It can be washed and stored in plastic bags in the refrigerator at about 40°F., ready for use as needed.

If you seem to have trouble with your favorite tossed green salad, perhaps you have been using lettuce that is not dry. The dressing will mix with the water remaining on the lettuce and run off into the bottom of the bowl, diluting the dressing so much that most of the flavor will be lost. Remember, lettuce should be fresh, crisp and dry. These three things will make a difference and improve your salad immeasurably.

The dressing should be at room temperature. If too cold it will cling to the lettuce, not dressing but smothering it. Have the bowl very cold and the lettuce chilled and this will chill the dressing.

Some interesting recipes for salads and salad dressings will follow but first here is the inevitable famous chef's Caesar salad so that if you are passionate about salads you can, after a considerable amount of practice, demonstrate your expertise before unbelieving friends.

57

salads

CAESAR SALAD

When my sister, Dorothy Hooker Nye, was director at Station KGO-TV in San Francisco, she had a cooking show on which there appeared many famous chefs as guests. One of her guests was the maitre d' at a renowned restaurant in San Francisco. I have enjoyed the excellent food there, and when Dorothy found out that I wanted the recipe for their Caesar salad, she asked and he gave it to her.

This is a very difficult salad to make, no matter how easy it looks when an expert does it at your table. The lettuce, and only romaine will do, no other will stand the number of tossings necessary in the making, must be very fresh, exceedingly cold and dry, dry, dry. Next, the manner of tossing the salad is most important. Follow the directions explicitly. You will have to experiment; and when you have found the proportions of everything, you will have something with which to astound your friends, confound your enemies and delight yourself every time you make the famous Caesar salad. And, most important, it must be made at the table, not ahead of time and brought on.

Into a bowl which is chilled in crushed ice, sitting in the ice itself, put **for each person: chopped romaine, cut across about 1/2 inch in width, about 1 cup**
Coddle in hot water for 1 minute, no longer:
1 whole egg
Break it right into the lettuce and toss. Add and toss some more:
juice of 1/2 lemon
Add:
paprika
sprinkle of salt
3 turns of fresh ground pepper, coarse
good dash of Worcestershire sauce
1/3 teaspoon dry English mustard for each 4 servings

Toss salad thoroughly again and add:
1-1/2 tablespoons olive oil in which garlic has been soaked and removed
1-1/2 tablespoons Parmesan cheese
Toss thoroughly for the last time. Serve, then place on each serving:
1 tablespoon small croutons
The classic, non-vegetarian version also calls for 1 or 2 anchovies. Notice that the ingredients are added in a certain order and the salad is thoroughly tossed at certain points in the procedure. This is very important to the final result. It may look easy, but your first few failures will prove it isn't. So follow directions exactly and may the blessings of all salad gods that watch over hardworking chefs be with you.

RAW VEGETABLE SALAD SUPREME

In the spring when, if you have a garden, new carrots, beets, turnips and the ever-present radishes are available, a colorful and very interesting salad can be made. Wash all vegetables well but do not peel them. Put them through the finest cone of a gricer to make long threads. If you do not have one a grater will do if it can make the long threads. First the turnips, then radishes then carrots and lastly the beets so you won't have to wash it between each using. On a plate which has been dressed with a bronze lettuce leaf, pile one mound each in a triangle, carrots, turnips and beets. In the center place the radishes. They are a bit peppery and your taste will have to determine the amount. Pass a bowl of sour cream garnish dressing that is slightly green from the addition of a few drops of coloring. This will bring many oohs and ahs from your guests.

salads

MARINATED RAW SPINACH SALAD

Mix together in these proportions a marinade:

1 cup fresh lemon juice
1 teaspoon salad herbs
1-1/2 teaspoons herb salt
1 cup olive oil

The spinach should be soaked and washed thoroughly to remove any trace of sand, then drained extra well so that no water remains to dilute the marinade. The marinating tends to act like a cooking agent on the spinach, removing just the right amount of rawness. For each portion use approximately:

1/2 cup spinach

Pour over the spinach enough dressing so that there is plenty in the bowl. Mix thoroughly and marinate for about 15 minutes, then drain thoroughly. For each serving put on a bed of lettuce:

shoestring beets, cooked and chilled
marinated spinach

Top with:

sour cream dressing
dash paprika
shredded red cabbage garnish

COOKED VEGETABLE SALAD

For those who for one reason or another will not or cannot eat raw foods the following salad is excellent. Using a vegetable peeler, prepare **very small carrots** and cut them in 1-inch lengths or if large ones, use them sliced thin. Cook until just tender and drain. (Vegetable water from all this preparation can be reserved for soup.)

Cook:

lima beans

until just done, also:

cauliflower, or
broccoli—
green beans—
niblet corn.

Mix all these vegetables together with **mayonnaise** which has been slightly thinned with **sour cream and a dash of garlic salt.**

Pile these vegetables on a lettuce-lined plate or in an unusually beautiful bowl. Alternate a garnish by laying strips of **shoestring beets** (which have been cooked, or canned and drained well) and long strips of: **Philadelphia-type cheese.** (Wrap a knife with a piece of paper that is used to wrap cubes of butter and cut the cheese so it will not stick to the knife.) Now dot the in-between places with sour cream garnish dressing (page 72).

BRANDIED RAISINS AND CARROT SALAD

Put into a jar that can be tightly covered and marinate for 1 week:

2 cups seedless raisins
1/4 cup good brandy
Mix the raisins with:
shredded carrots, to your taste
(some people prefer equal amounts) The marinated raisins do not have to be all used when the jar is opened. A small amount may be removed and the remainder saved. Mix in electric mixer:
1 cup mayonnaise
4 tablespoons crunchy peanut butter
3 tablespoons honey
1/2 cup sour cream
2 tablespoons vinegar
Mix to your taste the proper amount of this dressing and serve the raisins and carrots on:
lettuce leaves topped with grated fresh coconut.

61

salads

BUFFET SALAD

Recently I was in England helping to set up the vegetarian kitchen of Brockwood, a private school. Because we had young English girls as **femmes de cuisine** it was important to give them something they could prepare every day without further instruction— something that would provide variety without the necessity of extra teaching.

We prepared large bowls of **chilled lettuce and watercress; raw carrots, turnips and beets** were run through a gricer, making them into thin threads and each put into a separate bowl, and there were bowls of **hard boiled eggs and shredded cheddar cheese.** Platters were lined with: **bronze lettuce** and piled with thinly sliced **cucumbers**
zucchini
celery and cooked,
sliced mushrooms
tomato wedges

were placed between the piles of fresh vegetables. On a tray were bowls of several types of salad dressings, also olive oil and vinegar, so that everyone could make his own salad and vary it from day to day. This was so popular as the salad course that we never changed it except that sometimes we added a different mixed salad for special interest. The specialty might be fresh peas and cooked, cubed carrots and celery with mayonnaise; or it might be cooked cauliflower and carrots mixed with mayonnaise and topped with sliced beets. In some areas it is possible to get jicama imported from Mexico and this crisp vegetable makes a wonderful addition, peeled and cut into slices or strips. For a large family or for parties or groups of people this is an excellent way to provide a variety salad.

QUICK MEXICAN SALAD

This salad is a little change from the ordinary tossed green salad. If the ingredients are already in the kitchen, it is very easy to prepare.

Toss lightly together in a chilled salad bowl:
2 washed and chilled heads of Boston lettuce (or iceberg) torn into pieces
1 small can pimientoes cut into strips
1 small bottle of olives, stuffed or ripe ones (pitted)
1 small can of marinated artichoke hearts, quartered
1 cup shredded mild cheddar cheese
1 large avocado, peeled and sliced
Add and toss again lightly:
1/2 cup oil dressing (see page 71)
Serve with toasted tortillas, if available, or the commercial equivalent—Fritos—toasted corn bits, or any type of crisp cracker.

GUACAMOLE

Cut into small cubes:
1 large tomato, unpeeled
Add:
1 small onion, or two green ones with tops, chopped fine
2 seeded and washed green chilis, chopped fine
Grind in mortar; then mix well with tomato, onion and chilis:
1 teaspoon salt
1/2 teaspoon garlic salt
1/2 teaspoon MSG (optional)
8 silantro leaves (or 2 culantro leaves)
1/2 hour before serving, cut into 1/2-inch cubes and add to mixture:
2 large ripe avocados
(If added to the mixture too soon, the avocado will darken.)
Serve on lettuce leaves, garnished with pimiento.
Serves 4.

salads

ITALIAN SALAD

Many years ago, an Italian friend made a pizza for me and served it with the following salad. Cook:
green beans
until they are just done, but not mushy. They may be left whole, sliced or frenched. Slice:
raw large onions
very thin. Make a marinade with:
1 cup olive oil
1/2 cup lemon juice
2 tablespoons red wine vinegar
dash of sugar
pinch of marjoram
pinch of thyme
pinch of basil
pinch of black pepper
1/2 teaspoon salt
1/4 teaspoon garlic salt
Mix the marinade thoroughly (with a wire whip). In separate pans, pour some of the marinade over the beans and onions. Let stand for about 15 minutes so the marinade can thoroughly penetrate. If this is done properly the vegetables will absorb the flavor of the marinade, and it will not be usable again. Pile a small amount of the well-drained green beans on:
a bronze lettuce leaf (for color)
then about six or eight rings of onion. To garnish this cut:
strips of pimiento
and lay them across the top, or:
canned shoestring beets, drained
This is a most excellent salad to accompany any of the starches like spaghetti.

MANY BEAN SALAD

This is a very simple salad to make and very good if the entree is not to be too rich and heavy. It consists of as many varieties of beans as desired, all marinated in the same dressing described in the preceding recipe for bean and onion salad. Use red beans, pinto beans, garbanzo beans, etc. Soak them overnight and then cook them all together the next day in plenty of water so they will not stick or get gummy. Now cook some green beans, cut up or whole, until just done. They should not lose their color. Marinate them and lay them as you would stack cord wood (pile them up side by side) on each side of a lettuce-dressed plate. Marinate the other beans and drain them well. Place them in the middle of the plate between the green beans. Top with some finely chopped green onion tops and a bit of pimiento for color. Be sure all the beans are well drained so there is not a pool of dressing underneath when the salad is eaten.

POTATO SALAD WITH COUNTRY BOILED DRESSING

I can remember, when I was young and living in the middle west, mayonnaise as a product on the grocer's shelf was unknown. When it first appeared everyone said it was too oily, for we were accustomed to boiled salad dressings made without oil of any kind. Here is a boiled dressing that can be served hot over hot boiled, cubed and salted potatoes and chopped green onions; a delicious old-fashioned potato salad.

Mix in saucepan:
1 cup water
3 tablespoons sugar
4 tablespoons vinegar
3/4 teaspoon dry mustard
3/8 teaspoon salt
Beat into mixture:
1 egg
Bring to a boil and pour immediately over potatoes and onions.

WATERCRESS AND EGG SALAD

Here is another old-fashioned, delicious salad my English grandmother made, using the boiled dressing cold.
Wash and remove hard stems:
watercress
Mix in:
a green onion, chopped fine
Hardboil:
about 2 eggs for each cup of watercress
Slice the eggs into eighths, lengthwise, lay them on the watercress in an old-fashioned bowl and add the
chilled boiled dressing
Garnish with:
paprika and chopped parsley.

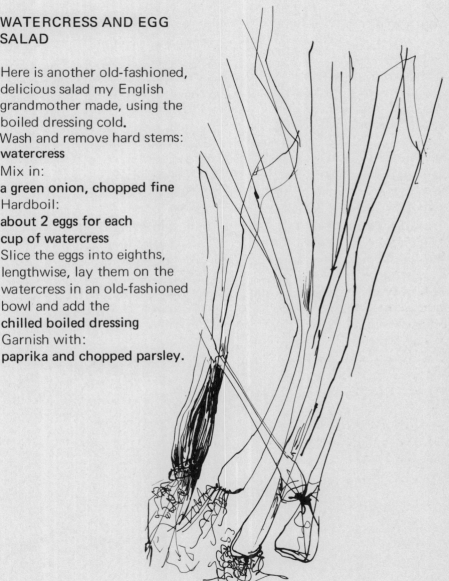

salads

BEET AND EGG SALAD PIQUANT

Threaded through Ohio is a group of recipes making a fabric of food and cooking habits that originally came from Pennsylvania Dutch whose background naturally did not include much fresh produce in the wintertime; they 'made do' with what was available. One of their delightful salads is still a very good change from the usual tossed green salad we are accustomed to. Remove tops, wash and cook in pressure cooker at 15 pounds for 15 minutes:

2 bunches small beets
2 cups water

Drain beets, reserving liquid, and when cool, remove skins. Add to beet juice, stirring in well:

2 tablespoons sugar
8 tablespoons vinegar (More or less according to taste)

Return beets to liquid and add:

6 (or more) eggs, hard-boiled and peeled

Put in refrigerator for at least 2 days so that the beet juice will penetrate the eggs. It will turn the whites a beautiful purple. To serve, using an egg slicer, slice the eggs and beets separately. Lay the slices in a neat pattern on a bed of bronze lettuce leaves; put dabs of sour cream garnish dressing (page 72) on the egg and beet slices and chopped pimineto on the dabs of dressing. Serve well chilled.

A VARIATION: Put a mound of cottage cheese on the lettuce, surround it with egg and beet slices, decorate with green garnish dressing, being careful not to cover the golden color of the egg yolks. Scatter on chopped pimiento.

PERSIMMON AND AVOCADO SALAD

About Christmas time in most states, since rapid transportation makes it possible, Japanese persimmons begin to appear in the market. Select them when they are nearly ripe if you are not planning to use them immediately, but do not refrigerate. During the ripening process the skin of the persimmon takes on a semi-transparency and it becomes quite soft to the touch. If the skin is not of this texture then the strong alum-like bitterness has not yet disappeared. Some people have said they do not like

persimmons because they are "puckery." This is because they have not had perfectly ripe ones.

At about the same time Fuerte avocados come in season. They are nut-like in flavor and the seed is not too large. These two delicacies are the foundation for this salad.

Gently grasp the ripe persimmon so as not to puncture it. If it is ripe enough this is the difficulty. As gently twist the dried stem end out (if it is still in). Stand the persimmon on a cutting surface with the point end up, and,

with a very sharp, thin, knife cut into four even quarters—in segments like an orange. Peel and cut the avocado into strips. Put a small mound of cottage cheese in the center of a lettuce leaf (bronze variety for color) on a plate and lay two quarters of the persimmon on each side. Lay strips of avocado on top of the persimmon. Top with Grenadine dressing (page 72).

Pomegranates are also in season and a few dark red seeds make a wonderful garnish on top of the pink dressing. An added touch is some shredded fresh coconut.

COMBINATION FRESH MELON SALAD

Peel as many types of melon as are available in the market. Slice them in strips lengthwise. Arrange them around a mound of cottage cheese on a bronze lettuce leaf. Top the cottage cheese with some Grenadine dressing (page 72). Sprinkle freshly grated coconut on top of the dressing and serve very cold.

BROILED PEACH SALAD

Place under broiler until good and hot:
cling peach halves
Lay on lettuce leaves pit side up and add:
chopped walnuts
Dribble over each half:
peanut butter dressing (page 72)

VARIATIONS OF BROILED PEACH SALAD

1. To make a very fancy salad, soak the peach halves in cognac before broiling.
2. Next to the hot peach half, put a small scoop of cold cottage cheese. The hot-and-cold combination is very interesting and delicious.
3. Fill the pit side of the peach with pineapple guava chutney (page 140), before broiling it. Topped with the peanut butter dressing this makes a very rich combination and should be served on the plate with the entree rather than as a salad.
4. Fill the peach with ginger sauce (page 173) before broiling. Serve without any other dressing except a sprinkling of freshly grated coconut.

PEACH SALAD

Place on lettuce leaf:
1/2 cooked peach
Fill center with:
1 teaspoon chopped candied ginger including the syrup
1 date, pitted and cut up
To make dressing, whip in mixer:
8 ounces Philadelphia cream cheese
When fluffy add:
1 ounce sweetened pineapple juice
1 ounce sour cream
Whip again for 1 minute. Place large spoonful of dressing on each peach, but do not cover it entirely. Place on top of dressing:
1/2 walnut meat, unbroken
Chill well before serving.

salads

SALAD DRESSINGS

A friend said, speaking of restaurant dining: "That ubiquitous baked potato—how I abhor it!" I feel that way about the salads offered in most restaurants—the equally ubiquitous salad, with choice of dressing; the waitress asking, "will you have French, Thousand Island or Roquefort dressing;" So, at the Ranch House we have tried to avoid the usual—and how far out we have gone you will have to decide for yourself. We like them; but then, we make them, and that may be the reason. However, our customers also like these dressings and that is very important in a restaurant operation.

WINE VINEGAR

To start off, here is a suggestion about wine vinegar. It is so easy and so simple and you can vary it as you wish, adding other herbs or varieties of wine. Sometimes a blend of wine makes an interesting flavor variation.

First, get a large wine bottle, dark glass preferably. Measure the following into it:
1 tablespoon tarragon, fresh if possible
4 cloves garlic, cut in quarters
2 quarts rich red wine
2 quarts cider vinegar, 5% acidity
Put this away in the dark for at least a week, a month is better, to age it. When ready to use, decant it and use as you would any wine vinegar.

FRENCH DRESSING

The simplest French dressing may after all be the very best. I have seen a waiter mix this one in the bottom of a well-chilled wooden bowl and then dump in sliced, ice-cold romaine or boston butter lettuce and just toss lightly. And what a salad it was, too!
Rub chilled wooden bowl with.
cut garlic clove
Add and mix:
1 part vinegar
2 parts olive oil
dash of salt
freshly ground black pepper

FRENCH DRESSING FOR FRUIT

Put in blender and mix
2 minutes:
1/2 cup water
1/2 cup cider vinegar, 5%
1/4 cup lemon juice
1 teaspoon salt
1 teaspoon capers
2 cloves garlic
1 tablespoon paprika
1/4 teaspoon MSG (optional)
1 teaspoon salad herbs
1 leaf fresh sage
6 leaves lemon verbena
1 cup peanut or other salad oil
For a more bland dressing
add more water.

PARSLEY FRENCH DRESSING FOR VEGETABLES

Put in blender and liquefy for
at least 2 minutes:
1-1/2 cups parsley tops
4 tablespoons vinegar, 5%
4 tablespoons water
3/4 cup lemon juice
2 tablespoons sherry
1/4 cup chives
or 2 green onions with tops
1 teaspoon dry mustard
1/2 teaspoon salt
1 teaspoon salad herbs
1 teaspoon herb salt
1/2 teaspoon black pepper,
fresh ground preferable
Add and blend for 1 minute:
2 tablespoons honey
1 cup peanut or other oil

UNUSUAL FRENCH DRESSING

Put in mortar and grind:
1 teaspoon salt
2 teaspoons paprika
1/2 teaspoon peppercorns
Add and grind again:
1/2 teaspoon dill seeds
1 teaspoon dry mustard
1/4 teaspoon celery seeds
1 teaspoon onion salt
Add and grind again:
3 cloves garlic, peeled
1/2 teaspoon MSG (optional)
Put in blender:
3/4 cup vinegar, 5%
1 cup peanut oil
2 tablespoons white sugar
3/4 cup water
2 tablespoons achioti oil
(optional)
Add ground spice and blend
for 2 minutes.

FRENCH OLIVE OIL DRESSING

Mix well together:
1 cup tarragon wine vinegar
1 teaspoon dry mustard
1/2 teaspoon fresh ground pepper
1/2 teaspoon salt
2 teaspoons herb salt
4 teaspoons paprika
1/2 teaspoon each,
oregano
basil
thyme
rosemary
More may be added if desired.
Add and mix or shake in
stoppered bottle:
2 cups olive oil at
room temperature

ROQUEFORT DRESSING

Mix thoroughly:
1 cup mayonnaise
2 to 4 ounces Roquefort cheese
1 cup table cream
1 teaspoon herb salt
1/2 teaspoon salad herbs

salads

5 Recipes

PINEAPPLE GUAVA AND CHEESE DRESSING

For fruit salads. Whip in mixer until very light:
1/2 pound Philadelphia cream cheese
Add and continue to whip until thoroughly blended:
1/4 cup chopped guavas, peeled
1 teaspoon creme de menth sauce (see dessert sauces)
sugar to taste
few drops green coloring (do not overcolor)

SOUR CREAM GARNISH DRESSING

Put into mixer and whip until thoroughly mixed:
1 pint sour cream
8 ounces Philadelphia cream cheese
2 teaspoons herb salt
1/3 cup parsley French dressing
3 drops green coloring

GRENADINE SOUR CREAM DRESSING

Once when I was whipping sour cream I became occupied with something else in the preparation of the meal, and allowed it to overwhip. It was only minutes before our guests were to arrive, and there was no time to get more sour cream! Out of desperation, I started grabbing and adding ingredients; and then I tasted it—and was delighted with the flavor of my concoction and used it on fresh fruit salad.

Put in mixer:
1 pint sour cream (sour whipping cream is best if available)
2/3 cup powdered sugar
2 tablespoons grenadine
4 tablespoons mayonnaise (optional)
2 ounces Philadelphia cream cheese
Whip until well mixed.

(2½ c)

SOUR CREAM DRESSING

Put into mixer and whip thoroughly:
1 pint sour cream (Real sour whipping cream is best but commercial type may be used)
1/2 cup mayonnaise
1 teaspoon onion salt
1/2 teaspoon garlic salt
1/4 teaspoon MSG (optional)
1/2 teaspoon salad herbs
2 ounces Philadelphia cream cheese

PEANUT BUTTER DRESSING

Whip in mixer:
1/4 cup peanut butter
1 cup mayonnaise
1/3 cup honey
3/4 cup coffee cream
1 tablespoon sauterne
1-1/2 tablespoons lemon juice
4 ounces cream cheese
pinch of salt
If too thick, thin with cream.

FRENCH DRESSING WITH GERANIUM LEAVES

Put in blender and run
for 2 minutes:
1-1/2 teaspoons herb salt
4 sprigs lemon thyme
1 sprig oregano
1 small sprig rosemary
1 leaf lemon geranium
1 leaf lime geranium
1 leaf nutmeg geranium
1 leaf apple geranium
1/2 leaf peppermint geranium
2 teaspoons paprika
1 teaspoon dry mustard
1 tablespoon white sugar
5 ounces vinegar, 5%
2 tablespoons water
Add and blend for 1 minute:
1 cup peanut oil or other salad oil

CUCUMBER DRESSING

For tossed green salad. Put
in blender and run for
2 minutes:
1/2 cucumber, unpeeled
1-1/2 teaspoons herb salt
1/16 teaspoon fresh ground
pepper
1/4 cup vinegar
1/2 cup sour cream
dash white sugar

73

salads

BANANA SALAD DRESSING

For fruit salads. Whip in
mixer for 3 minutes:
4 ounces cream cheese
2 ripe bananas
3 tablespoons honey
3 tablespoons sour cream
1/2 cup coffee cream
1 tablespoon lemon juice
1/16 teaspoon ground cardamon
seed

POPPY SEED DRESSING

For fruit salads. Put in
blender and run for 2 minutes:

1-1/2 cups vinegar (cider, 5%)
2 tablespoons paprika
1/2 teaspoon black pepper
1 tablespoon salad herbs
2 teaspoons poppy seeds
1-1/2 teaspoons salt
Add and blend 1 minute:
10 tablespoons honey
1-1/2 cups peanut oil
1 tablespoon herb salt
3 large costmary leaves,
they are like mint
4 leaves pineapple sage
2 leaves fresh woodruff
1/2 teaspoon grated ginger root

breads

HOME MADE MIRACLES OF BREAD

In a vegetarian diet, bread is basic. Wheat is almost a complete food in itself. In order to make good bread, something should be known about the ingredients that are to be used.

Bread flour is of two types mainly—soft winter wheat flour and hard spring wheat flour. The softness or hardness can be detected by rubbing a pinch of flour between thumb and forefinger; soft flour feels silky soft and hard flour feels gritty.

Soft flour has less gluten and therefore the structure of its dough is weaker. This is the dough used for cake, cookie and pie crust baking where toughness is not desirable. Hard flour, the harder the better, is used for Vienna and French breads and it is largely their toughness which gives these breads their splendid character.

There are usually two types of yeast—the cake type which can be bought at a grocery or in one pound bricks at a bakery, and the dry yeast which comes in little packets. Cake yeast is ready for use. The dry type must be reconstituted, but this does not take too long, just long enough for it to start its growth, about 15 minutes.

Yeast, during its period of growth, consumes food which is usually sugar or honey. The by-products are water and carbon dioxide gas which is the rising faculty it gives the dough. The best temperature for the growth of the yeast is the normal temperature of the human body; therefore, in setting the dough aside to rise, it must be kept at about this temperature. The dough should be covered with a dry cloth so the top will not dry out and form a crust.

In the old days, bread makers scalded the milk before using it in making bread. This was

75

breads

done to kill off undesirable types of yeast that had collected in the milk from the air, which always carries what is called "wild yeast." This "wild yeast" produces all sorts of molding and souring in foods. Millions of dollars have been spent by processors of commercial yeast to isolate one particular strain of tough, durable and hardy yeast that will do the best work in raising the bread dough. If other types of yeast are present, the rising time of the dough will be unpredictable. Commercially, it is desirable to have a standardized yeast, the use of which will produce the same result over and over. Also, this type of yeast will stand more heat and cold before being killed and will grow faster than other varieties. If cake yeast is used, freshness is important. (If cake yeast is slightly brown when you take it out of the wrapping, it probably is still good.) Dry yeast, reconstituted with lukewarm water and sugar, is excellent and easier to find in most grocery stores. The gluten in the flour is what

makes a paste that is tough enough to hold the bubbles of gas released by the growth of the yeast.

Some doughs are raised with baking powder or baking soda. Even pie dough rises a little, if handled correctly. This rising produces the flakes which are so desirable in good pie crust.

Unless the type of bread is unusual there should be two risings. After the dough has been mixed and set aside for the first rising—to double its bulk—then it is punched down, the air knocked out of it so that it can be divided into loaves, kneaded, molded and put into the pans. Then it is again set in a warm place, covered with a cloth and allowed to rise to double its bulk. It will rise some in the oven but not enough to make a too light loaf.

Using very little liquid other than water will give the best texture to a loaf of bread, but such fine texture is gained at

the expense of flavor. Butter, milk and sweetening (more than the yeast needs for its growth) are used to get the delicious flavor we look for in home made bread.

The difference in the cost of butter as compared to that of vegetable shortening or margarine is so slight that, unless one is on a low cholesterol diet, it seems foolish to use any substitute for it. For whole milk there is an acceptable substitute in powdered milk, which can be reconstituted according to the directions on the package and used in place of fresh milk in any recipe.

A simple fact to keep in mind: Salt deters the action of yeast and tends to stabilize and control its growth and raising power in bread. If the bread rises too fast in room temperature (72°–75°), perhaps the recipe does not call for enough salt or the salt is not being mixed with the yeast and sweetening.

76

For the beginner, kneading the dough should not be a difficult task. All that is meant by the word is that the dough should be pushed down with both hands, then flattened so that it can be folded over and pushed down again—that is kneading. This develops the gluten content in the flour—the part that is rubbery and that makes it possible for the bubbles of gas to blow up and expand and raise the dough. Pushing and pulling the dough causes the gluten to absorb water (reconstitute itself). When properly kneaded the dough should be smooth and soft and rubbery.

A warm place must be found for the rising of the bread, such as the top of a gas range where the pilot light is going. Care must be taken that the bottom of the bread pan gets no hotter than the top, or the bread will rise unevenly, making the texture of the loaf uneven so that when slicing it will crumble and break.

Some people like to butter the top of the bread just after it comes from the oven. I find this makes the loaves unpleasantly greasy to handle. To make a butter crust as the loaf bakes, cut a long, shallow slash in the center of the loaf just before baking and lay in a very thin slice of butter. An old lady who was an excellent baker said that bread should feel "as warm and soft as a baby's bare behind," and this is the best description I have found. The temperature of the ingredients and the room where the bread is being made will have a definite effect on the rising time of the dough, varying it from twenty-five minutes to an hour. In summer the dough has to be protected from excessive heat. In mixing, if the flour is cold, the liquid should be correspondingly warmer than usual. These are things experience will teach you to watch for as you mix and knead and bake your loaves.

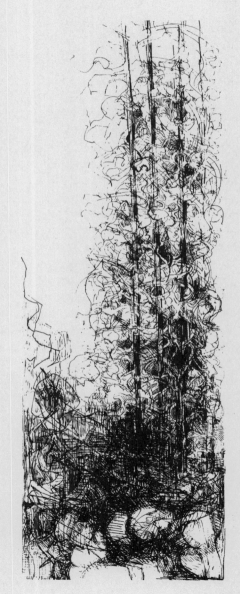

breads

WHOLE WHEAT BREAD

The story of the development of our whole wheat bread is interesting, I think, and typical of many of the methods and recipes still in use at the Ranch House, with improvements added through experience.

When we moved to Ojai it was with the intention of making everything we could, growing everything we could and in every way avoiding all types of process and 'tampered with' foods. The idea of having a cow and fresh milk from her soon went out the window, for the man who owned the cow on the ranch where we first lived told us that he had kept books on the milk production and could have bought the milk for the price he paid for the feed and cost of maintaining the cow, not counting the twice daily milking chore. So . . .

But we had our own garden, and our experiment with natural living began. I started making whole wheat bread and it did taste very good. The owner of

78

the health food store asked me to bring some loaves for him to sell and charged me no commission on his sales. He also suggested that I use stone ground meal instead of the graham flour I was using, and I began experimenting with the recipe. After many months I came to understand the properties of this meal and the resulting loaf was excellent. Everyone loved it and soon many were buying loaves to take home after they had dined with us.

Demand for the bread increased and it was becoming physically impossible to do the gardening, cooking, pastry and bread making along with all the other things that are connected with running a restaurant. A friend in Santa Barbara brought me an old-fashioned bread mixer, the type that fastened to the table and had a handle at the top to turn. This was fine but I still had to turn the handle! I looked around for some mechanical assistance. We had an old washing machine from which I intended to remove and sell the motor. I began

thinking about how I could attach that motor to the handle of the bread mixer; then an idea struck me—why not convert the washing machine itself into a bread mixer? I called a machinist who took the washing machine and stopped the drain with a stainless steel plug, removed the wringer and filled the bottom of the agitator with metal so that it would be easy to clean and we were in business!

When I started using the machine I did not know that this method would make an entirely different loaf of bread because it would undermix the dough. The walls of the bubbles in the dough would be thicker and so a flavor of undeveloped gluten would be baked into the loaf and a heavier loaf with a coarser texture and much more flavor would result. (I had always wondered why most commercial bread has so little flavor. Most bakeries are interested in producing a high, soft, light loaf of bread. The shopper, picking up such a soft loaf will feel it and think

that it must be fresh. This
may be so but the loaf is also
without much flavor.) As Lili
Kraus once said when she was
given a fresh, hot slice, "it
is actually old-time peasant
bread!" A lighter loaf, though
it may be twice the size, will
have only half the flavor. In
all our breads flavor comes
first, texture and lightness
second.

Whole wheat, and the reference
here is to stone ground wheat
flour, contains the entire
wheat berry with nothing taken
away or added to it. It is
crushed between stone burrs
and ground slowly so that the
wheat germ oil is pressed into
the flour, not lost on the
machinery or vaporized by heat
generated by the speed of steel
rollers.

Because of the amount of bran
and other coarse outside parts
of the wheat berry in this
flour, it takes a high amount
of gluten of good, tough quality
to hold the dough firm so that
in the rising process the little
bubbles caused by the action of

breads

the yeast will not burst; if these little bubbles burst they make holes in the bread. If too much of this bubble bursting takes place the inside of the loaf is too porous and heavy. The flour must make a dough that will hold together and not break easily when stretched. This is important for texture as well as flavor.

White or brown sugar are adequate sweeteners but honey gives more flavor and tends to keep the bread from drying out. Molasses is sometimes used for sweetening and it is excellent for those who like it, though it does tend to mask the true flavor of the wheat. There are recipes that call for about four times the amount of honey we use in our recipe. This also masks the true wheat flavor. These variations are a matter of individual taste, giving you a chance to develop your own special recipe.

Wheat is grown in various parts of the country and in different soils. Some is harder and some softer because

of these conditions. If the dough seems inclined to be too sticky maybe it needs a slight increase in the amount of flour over that previously used, even though the flour is the same brand and purchased from the same supplier. Add or hold back only a small amount, a few tablespoons as an experiment, if the dough does not handle properly.

As a variation, wheat germ can be added to the recipe without changing the texture. This is done by substituting one ounce of wheat germ for one ounce in each pound of flour used. Soy flour is sometimes added but because of the high quantity of oil and lack of gluten in it, it can be added only in small quantities without seriously changing the texture of the loaf. If you wish to experiment, substitute about ten per cent to begin with and add more in small amounts until you get the desired loaf.

Nutritionists say that the whole wheat berry contains

a wonderful array of vitamins and minerals. The importance of this is for the individual to decide.

Now for the recipe. It may not be the best in the world but it has found favor with those who have bought and eaten it in Southern California for some years.

RANCH HOUSE STONE GROUND WHOLE WHEAT BREAD

Using a metal pan which can be warmed, mix together:

1/2 cup warm water
2-1/4 cups milk
1 tablespoon butter
1/3 cup honey
2 teaspoons salt

Heat to 90°—about body temperature—add and stir in well:

2 packages dry yeast

Let stand until yeast dissolves and bubbles begin to appear—little ones. Then add and mix in well, first with a spoon then by hand to get in all the four:

6-2/3 cups sieved whole wheat flour

(5-3/4 cups unsieved flour equals 6-2/3 cups sieved flour. Accurate measurements are important.) Knead until thoroughly mixed. It should be moist and slightly sticky Cover with a cloth and set in a warm place. Let rise to double its bulk (15 to 20 minutes). Turn out onto a floured board and knead again for at least 10 minutes, pressing it down flat, folding it over and turning it around until all the large air bubbles are squeezed out. This is to make a good texture. Dough should be springy to the touch, good and tough.

Mold into loaves, thus: cut dough into two equal pieces; flatten each piece out and fold over, doing this again and again until, when rolled up it will make a 'log' the size of the bread pan. Have the pans well greased with shortening—butter burns off and lets the bread stick. When the dough is put in the pan be sure that the upper surface is smooth and unbroken, for this is to be the top of the loaf and should not have a break which would let the dough break out in a bubble. Let rise until dough is about 1 inch higher than the pan. Bake for 45 minutes at 375°. Turn out on rack to cool.

A few comments. If the dough is allowed to rise too long the first time it will be sticky, impossible to handle without drenching the board with flour. This additional flour will dry out the dough and make a dry loaf. If the dough is too "young," as the expression goes in the baking business, it will not be springy enough and will take too long to rise the second time. When making the "log," seal the two edges together and lay this seam side in the bottom of the pan. Fruit and/or nuts can be added to this dough as it is being mixed. Walnuts, pecans, sunflower seeds, shredded fresh coconut, cashews, or a cup or two of raisins, currants or pitted dates—all of these give wonderful flavor and texture. Also, if it is available to you, fresh coconut milk is a wonderful substitute for cow's milk. What a flavor, with the addition of the freshly grated coconut! What fun you can have experimenting with these various combinations!

breads

WHOLE RYE BREAD

It seems impossible to find in any store a loaf of bread made of all rye flour. Here is a recipe for one that will surprise you with its excellent flavor. Mix well together:

1-1/4 cups warm whole milk
3/4 cup warm water
2 tablespoons butter (1 ounce)
2 tablespoons molasses
2 tablespoons honey
2 teaspoons salt
Keeping the mixture lukewarm, add and mix in well:
2 packages dry yeast
1-1/2 tablespoons caraway seeds (optional but excellent)
Let stand until yeast starts to bubble a little then add and mix in:
2-1/2 cups rye flour
Continue to mix then again add and mix in well:
2-1/2 cups rye flour
Unless you have a Kitchen Aid mixer with a dough hook for bread making you will have to get in with your hands to mix this dough thoroughly. Yes, it is very sticky and messy but pay no attention to that—the end result will be worth it. There is very little gluten in rye flour and it must all be developed by mixing.

When mixed, cover with cloth and let stand in warm place to rise to double its bulk, about one hour. Turn out onto floured board and knead for at least 5 minutes. Divide into 2 loaves. Prepare as directed in Whole Wheat Bread recipe. Put into well greased pans, 7½ x 3½, and let rise again, but not as high as the whole wheat dough or it will fall in the oven. There is not enough gluten in the dough to hold it up that high. Bake at 360° for 40 minutes. Remove from oven and brush tops of loaves with butter. Place on cooling rack.

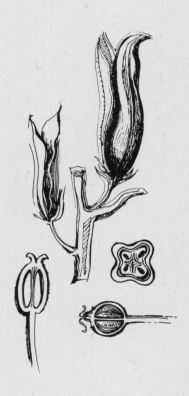

SESAME-SOYA BREAD

Mix together and heat to
lukewarm, about 90°:
1 cup whole milk
1 tablespoon butter
1/4 cup wheat germ
1/2 cup soya flour
2 teaspoons salt
1/4 cup honey
3/4 cup water
Add to lukewarm mixture and
stir in well:
2 packages dry yeast
Let stand for 10 minutes, then
using a large spoon add:
**2-1/2 cups sifted, white,
unbleached flour**
When flour is all mixed in, add
and continue to mix:
2-1/2 cups sifted flour,
same as above
Put dough into a bowl, cover
with cloth and set in a warm
place to rise to double its
bulk. This first rising will
take 1-1/2 to 2 hours.

Turn out on floured board and
knead for at least 10 minutes.
Divide into 2 pieces. Prepare
as directed in Whole Wheat
Bread recipe. Coat top of
loaves with a mixture of:
egg white and a little water
using a pastry brush. Now
sprinkle the top with:
raw sesame seeds.
Let rise to about 1 inch above
edge of pan then bake at 360°
for 40 minutes or until nicely
brown. Turn out onto cooling
rack.

RAISIN BREAD

This bread is easy to make.
Simply add 2 cups of raisins
to the soya bread dough. Do not
add seeds to the top of the
loaf. When the bread comes out
of the oven, glaze it with
powdered sugar
mixed in a little water. The less
water, the thicker the coating.

breads

GERMAN FRUIT BREAD

Mix and warm gently, to about
90°, stirring constantly
until butter is melted:
1 tablespoon butter
1-1/2 cups whole milk
2 tablespoons soya flour
1/2 cup honey
3/4 teaspoon salt
Add and stir until dissolved:
2 packages dry yeast, or
3 cakes fresh yeast
If using dry yeast, let stand
for 15 minutes.
Beat lightly and add:
1 egg
Add and mix in well:
2 cups sifted white bread flour
Then add and mix in:
2-3/4 cups white bread flour

Dredge:
1/2 pound candied fruit
in 1/2 cup flour
Add to fruit, but do not dredge
with flour:
1-1/2 cups walnuts
Then mix nuts and fruit into
dough. Allow dough to rise
until double its bulk, 2 to
3 hours. Knead again and divide
into 2 pieces. Prepare as
directed in Whole Wheat Bread
recipe. Allow to rise again to
nearly double its bulk. Bake
at 350° for 40 minutes.
Remove from oven and glaze with
a mixture of:
powdered sugar and water
to make a white coating. Use
a thick mixture for a thick
glaze. Place on cooling rack.

DATE NUT BREAD

Put together in small pan
or bowl:
5 ounces pitted, chopped dates
2-1/2 tablespoons butter
1/2 teaspoon salt
Pour over dates and let stand
10 minutes:
1-1/4 cups boiling water
Mix well together:
1 egg
1-1/4 cups white sugar
Sift well together:
1-7/8 cups bread flour
**1/2 teaspoon Calumet baking
powder**
1-1/2 teaspoons baking soda
Stir together the date mixture
and the egg mixture, add these
to the flour mixture and beat
in well, using electric mixer.
Add and mix in well:
1-1/2 cups chopped walnuts
1 teaspoon vanilla

Pour into 2 loaf pans, 7-1/2 x
3-1/2, lined with brown paper
that has been brushed with
shortening. Bake at 375° for
45 to 50 minutes or until the
top rises up and cracks a little.
Unless this crack appears the
inside is not completely baked.
When done, remove from pan,
place on cooling rack.

OATMEAL BREAD

Cook in double boiler for
30 minutes:
1 cup old fashioned oatmeal
1 cup water
Remove to mixing bowl and add,
mixing in well:
2 tablespoons butter
1-1/2 teaspoons salt
5 tablespoons honey
Mix together and soak for
15 minutes:

1/2 cup warm milk
2 packages dry yeast
Add yeast mixture to oatmeal and
mix, then add and mix in well:
**3 tablespoons hulled sunflower
seeds**
3 tablespoons chopped walnuts
1 cup white bread flour
Add and knead in to the correct
consistency, about 10 minutes:
2-1/4 cups white bread flour
Let rise to double the bulk
then shape into loaves and put
into well-greased bread pans,
size 7-1/2 x 3-1/2.   Let rise
again but not too high, as it
will sink in the oven because
of the oatmeal in the dough—not
enough gluten in it.
To decorate top of loaves,
brush them with a mixture of:
egg white and a little water,
then sprinkle with:
raw rolled oats.
Bake at 375° for 45 to 50 minutes.

breads

PARKER HOUSE ROLLS

At home, our birthdays,
holidays and any special days
were always celebrated by making
wonderful, fragrant and
delicious rolls named for the
famous inn of long ago—the
Parker House in Boston. It is
well worth the little bit of
extra work it takes to make
them. Try some—you will be
delighted as we always were.
Mix together:
1 cup warm milk
1/2 package dry yeast
4 tablespoons white sugar
Let mixture stand for about
20 minutes to reconstitute,
then add and mix well:
1-1/2 teaspoons salt
4 tablespoons melted butter
2 cups white flour
Add and mix in:
1 egg
Add and continue to mix:
2 cups white flour
Cover with cloth and let dough
rise to double its bulk. Turn
out on floured board and smooth
dough to about 1/2-inch
thickness, then cut with small
biscuit cutter into rounds.
Crease each round with dull
edge of a knife, putting the
crease just a little off center.
Brush the smaller side with
butter and fold it over the
larger side. Place rolls in
pan far enough apart to prevent
their touching one another. Let
rise until double in bulk, then
bake at 400° for 15 to 20
minutes until nicely browned on
top. Yields about twenty-two
2-1/2-inch rolls.

POTATO MUFFINS

Mix together and let stand
for 5 hours:
**3 small potatoes, boiled and
put through ricer**
1 teaspoon salt
1 teaspoon shortening
1 tablespoon butter
1 tablespoon sugar
2 well-beaten eggs
1/3 package dry yeast soaked in
1 cup lukewarm milk
**4 cups white flour, enough to
make a stiff dough**
Roll out dough, shape into
muffins. Let rise for 2 hours.
Bake at 425° for about 10
minutes. Should make 36 muffins.

WAFFLES

Place in mixing bowl:
2 cups sifted cake flour
2 tablespoons sugar
Add and mix in lightly:
1 cup milk
1/4 cup cold water
Beat, then add:
3 egg yolks
1/2 teaspoon salt
Then add:
6 tablespoons melted butter
Mix well, then add and mix
again:
3 teaspoons Royal baking powder
Fold in:
**3 egg whites, whipped stiff but
not dry**
1/2 teaspoon salt
Whipping the eggs with the salt
stiffens them without making
them dry. The steps in this
recipe are very important and
should be followed just as they
are given. This makes a light
batter which will hold up until
the last waffle is cooked. Do
not grease the griddle. Serve
with melted butter and hot
maple syrup, or maple butter
made by combining butter with
maple syrup and beating it well
together.

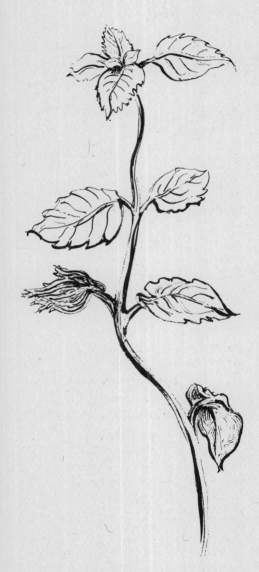

NOBODY INFLUENCES ME!

I am periodically
besieged by one or another of the
multitude of food faddists.
I seem especially to attract
every crackpot with a real food
neurosis.

One day, after a particularly
deadly onslaught complete with
reasons why I should eat in what
they call the "health way,"
with great glee I set out to make
a concoction that I knew was
going to be so horrible that
even the most dedicated faddist
could not stomach it. I put
together everything I had ever
heard of that would bring
dynamic, vibrant, radiant,
bubbling, creative, irritating
good health, and then put this
potential dynamite into a muffin
tin and baked it.

I have to report that those
muffins turned out to have a
marvelous flavor and gave a
quite noticeable jolt of energy.
But nobody is going to influence
me, and I can resist their ideas
by refusing to make these
abundantly delicious bits of good
health. However, there is no
reason why you should not try
them, so go to the health food
store and buy the ingredients.

ATOMIC MUFFINS

Put into mixing bowl:
1/2 cup soya or safflower oil
3/4 cup brown sugar
2 tablespoons blackstrap molasses
2 eggs
Mix, then add and mix again:
1 teaspoon salt
3/4 cup wheat germ
1/4 cup soya flour
1/2 cup powdered milk
1/2 cup sesame meal
1/2 cup brewers' yeast
1 cup whole wheat flour,
stone ground
1/2 cup whole sunflower seeds
1-1/2 cups milk
2-1/2 teaspoon Royal baking
powder
Add and mix again:
1 cup raisins
1 cup nut meats
1/8 cup rolled oats,
old-fashioned type
Bake in muffin tins, 18 minutes
at 375°.
Makes about 24 muffins.

breads

QUICK COFFEE CAKE

This recipe is really just that—quick. We were invited to tea by three charming elderly ladies. After a few minutes one of them excused herself and not too long afterward came back with a freshly baked coffee cake on the tea tray. I was so delighted with it I asked for the recipe and here it is. Try it when someone drops in and you don't have a thing in the house to serve.

It can be done in 35 minutes—10 minutes for mixing and about 25 minutes for baking.

Cream together:
1/2 cup sugar
2 tablespoons melted butter
Mix together and add:
1 egg
1 cup whole milk
Mix together and add, mixing lightly:
1-1/4 cups bread flour
2 teaspoons Royal baking powder
1/4 teaspoon salt
Do not overmix, as it will get too tough. Spread evenly in a 9-inch, well-greased cake pan equipped with bottom cutter to

88

help in removing the cake while it is still hot. Sprinkle lightly with:
cinnamon and sugar, mixed (1/4 part cinnamon, 3 parts sugar)
1/4 cup chopped nuts
Bake at 425° for about 20 to 25 minutes or until nicely brown. Cut and serve while hot.

LUXURY CORN BREAD

Mix well together:
1-1/2 cups yellow cornmeal
1/2 cup white flour
1/4 cup sugar
1/2 teaspoon soda
1 teaspoon salt
1/2 cup raisins (optional but delicious)
Beat together and add, mixing well but lightly:
1 egg
1-1/4 cups sour cream, or,
1 cup milk and
1/4 cup melted butter
Pour into well-greased shallow 9-inch pan and bake at 425° for 20 to 25 minutes. This bread can be split when cold and toasted and then drenched with melted butter, just to make it extra rich and delicious.

SCOTCH SCONES

Mix together with pastry blender and then by hand until as fine as cornmeal:
4 cups white flour
2 teaspoons cream of tartar
1-1/2 teaspoons baking soda
1 teaspoon salt
6 tablespoons butter
Add and mix well:
6 tablespoons white sugar
Mix together, then add to the above and just mix in (Too much mixing will toughen the dough):
1-1/2 cups buttermilk
2 eggs
Drop by spoonfuls onto greased cookie sheet, or pour into two well-greased cake tins. Baking time, 8 to 10 minutes, at 400°, or until nicely brown on top. Because of the sugar in the batter, the scones tend to burn on the bottom if they are left in the oven too long. They can be slit open when cold and toasted and buttered. Recipe makes about 36 large scones.

rice and grains

A CHEF'S WAY WITH RICE AND GRAINS

The northern peoples of the world are, as a rule, wheat eaters; the southern folks are rice eaters. Because of climatic conditions this is surely a most natural thing; wheat is the grain of the cool north, rice the grain of the warm south. More than two-thirds of the world's people use rice as a major part of their diet; consider the millions in Japan, India and China.

In serving this wonderfully nourishing starch keep in mind that it is mostly just that— rich starch. A few other hints may be of value to you as you experiment with rice cooking. Wheat and rice are dried seeds and the cooking process reconstitutes them for human consumption. They must be made to re-absorb the moisture that went out of them as they ripened for harvesting.

Authorities say there are more than fifty varieties of rice. For our rice dishes we will

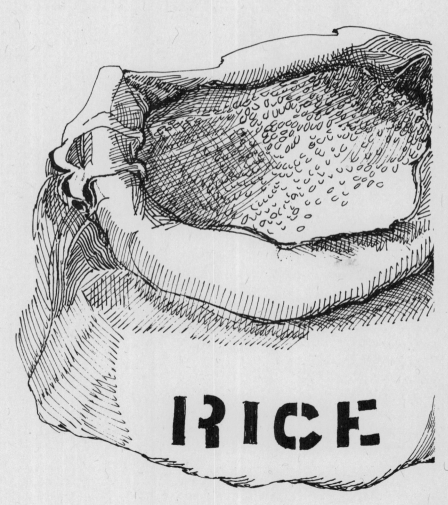

RICE

rice and grains

suggest only the three familiar categories—white, brown and wild rice. Actually, the last named one is not a rice; it is a cereal gathered by the northern American Indians. They harvest it by knocking it into their canoes as they paddle along the shores of American and Canadian lakes where it grows. The cereal is also the main food of wild ducks. A limit has been set on the amount of wild rice that can be gathered, and the Indians have the sole right to harvest it. It is an important part of their diet and this explains why there is such a small amount that reaches the market and why its price is so high.

White rice is natural brown rice with the outside covering removed by a process called polishing. Nutritionists say the outside covering is rich in the vitamin B complex and do not recommend the use of polished rice but many people prefer white rice, depending on other foods and vitamin pills for their supply of the vital B complex vitamins.

There are two main methods of cooking rice: the Chinese and the Turkish or Near Eastern. The Chinese way is to slowly introduce the rice into a pot of rapidly boiling salted water, so that the water will not stop boiling as the rice is added. The rice is cooked until tender, usually about 20 minutes, and is then poured into a large strainer, to drain. Hot water is run over it to wash away the starch that comes out in the cooking. The rice is then put in a pan and into the oven to reheat before serving. This method keeps the rice from being sticky and makes it nice and fluffy. (There are so-called quick-cooking brands

of rice on the market. Personally, I do not like these 'pre-fabricated' time savers—they do not have the right flavor. To me, they taste something like a poor variety of wet popcorn.)

The other method of cooking rice is to put oil or butter in a pan that can be tightly covered and when it has melted, stir in unwashed rice and the salt. The pan is then put over a very hot flame until the grains begin to look a little white. Immediately boiling water is poured over the rice and it is stirred and covered, then put over low heat to simmer. The proper method is to get the rice as hot as possible without browning it at all, so that when the water is added it will continue to boil up vigorously until the cover is put on. The heat is then turned to simmer, so as not to evaporate the water. If this method is followed correctly, all the water will have been absorbed by the rice when it is done. It will be fluffy, with little holes like tiny volcanos scattered through it. Never under any

circumstances should the rice be stirred after the water is added. Stirring will break up the structure of the cooking rice grains which seem to form themselves together and to lift up the entire mass. Rice cooked this way can be kept in the pan over a warm burner with a couple of asbestos pads under it for at least an hour without losing too much of its goodness and texture.

Either of these methods may be used in cooking wild rice. Some people may not like its extra strong flavor. To get rid of this, using the washed rice method, cook it about twenty minutes, drain it, then continue as with the white rice. Wild rice needs something strong to complement its dominant flavor.

Rice is included in this chapter on the cereal grains, for even if there is controversy about its being a grain, it is cooked the same way and often served the same way; and so-called wild rice is a grain.

rice and grains

GRAINS

Grains provide a good source of protein, so important in the vegetarian diet. They are easily prepared and delicious served plain or with vegetables and herbs for flavor.

The simplest method of cooking grains seems to be the one that provides the most flavor—practically the same method used in cooking rice: boiling water added to the grain after it has been heated in a pan or kettle that has a tight fitting lid, with or without the addition of salt and oil or butter. A little of the boiling water should be added at first so it will not boil over, then add the remainder and do not let it stop boiling; this is important. Cover immediately and turn to low heat and let it simmer. Don't let it stop bubbling slightly, but it should not boil hard as that will evaporate the water before the grain is reconstituted and it will be hard and inedible.

The package usually tells how long to cook the grain but a good rule is to let it cook for at least half an hour before looking at it. By no means remove the cover before then and let out the steam! Also, **don't stir the grain during the cooking process.** As it cooks the expanding kernels push each other up to form a network. If this structure is broken before the grain is completely cooked it becomes a soggy mess that is unpalatable. After it is cooked it can be stirred, other things can be added—it doesn't matter. It can be stored in the refrigerator and reheated the next day in a covered pan with the addition of a little water. But all of this after it has been thoroughly cooked.

Here are suggestions for cooking and serving the various grains:

BROWN RICE

1 cup brown rice
2 cups boiling water
Follow the cooking method suggested here and cook for at least 1 hour. Sometimes the variety that comes from the Chico people takes longer— perhaps 15 minutes more—before it is really well cooked. Serve topped with onion butter (page 20).

MILLET

1 cup millet
four cups boiling water
Cook for at least 30 minutes before removing the lid, then try for doneness; tastes differ about this. Top with pimiento and green pepper butter (page 20).

BULGAR WHEAT

The simplest way to cook this grain is to put the water in the pan (2 cups water for 1 cup of Bulgar), bring it to boil and add the grain and 1 teaspoon salt. Cook covered for about 20 minutes or until it is done to your taste. Top with garlic butter (page 20).

STEEL CUT OATS

Cook this grain the same way as the Bulgar, except that it needs a little more water added after about 20 minutes. When done properly it will have a delicious crust on the bottom. After it has cooked for a while it must be gently stirred, for it does not form the structure the other grains do; by nature it is too sticky for this.

rice and grains

SPROUTING GRAINS

You might be interested in experimenting with something the so-called health-minded people use (What an expression! As if only certain people were interested in health!). Select a small pyrex or other glass dish that can be covered. Lay four thicknesses of paper toweling on the bottom. Soak 1/2 cup of any grain or seeds such as whole wheat, alfalfa, soya beans, mustard, cress, in one cup of lukewarm water for a half hour. Drain off enough water so that when you pour the seeds into the bowl they will not float.

Every day add a cup more water and drain off the excess. In five days usually, you will have sprouts ready to eat. These sprouts are delicious used in fresh salads—filled with 'vital electricity' they say. Maybe they are! Anyhow, I love the fresh crunchy taste of them.

Use your own sprouting arrangement if you can find a better way than the one I have described. In Switzerland they have a very elegant gadget called a Bio Snacky. It is made by Samen Mauser in Zurich. It has four levels with a hole in each of the top three so the water can run down. With it three different types of grain can be sprouting at the same time.

94

INDONESIAN RICE

Cook in the recommended way:
2 cups rice
4 tablespoons butter
1 teaspoon salt
In pressure cooker without cap
and using very little water,
put vegetables in layers in
this order:
1/2 cup carrots sliced in thin
2-inch strips
1/2 cup celery, sliced very
thin in 2-inch strips
1/2 cup green beans, french-cut
in thin 2-inch strips
1/2 teaspoon savory herb blend
Cook about 2 minutes, drain
and add:
butter enough to thoroughly
coat vegetables
Add vegetables to rice and toss
until mixed, then sprinkle on
generously:
natural sliced almonds (with
skin left on).
Hot but not browned pine nuts
may be added to vegetables or
sprinkled on as garnish. Cashews
alone may be used, but not with
other nuts. They make an
excellent variation.

This combination of rice and
vegetables is the center of one
type of "rijsttafel" served
in Indonesia and Java. By
spreading the rice on a large
platter and arranging all manner
of vegetables around it and
garnishing the rice with the
nuts, one can make this the
main dish of a buffet luncheon
or dinner.

JAVANESE RICE

An unusually fine cook who was
born in Java of Dutch parents
and lived many of her young
years there used to prepare
rice in the following way. She
would cook her rice in the
regulation manner—using plenty
of boiling water—then rinse off
the extra starch, drain it and
dump it into a large saucepan.
To this she would add the
following ingredients:
For 3 cups of cooked rice)
1 small can of inch-long green
beans.
(She was able to get what are
called three foot beans. They

are a very thin pencil bean an
a little on the crispy side
instead of being mushy.)
1 large onion, thinly sliced
cooked in butter
until completely done, but not
mushy. For an extra touch she
would sometimes add some raisins
sprinkled on top.

The rice would be lightly
tossed with the beans and onions
and gently reheated at serving
time. Sometimes it would be
served nearly cold but we, who
do not eat with our fingers as
some of the orientals do, prefer
our food slightly hotter.

rice and grains

RICE SPECIALE — INDIA

Using Chinese method, prepare
light and fluffy:
2 cups rice
1 teaspoon salt
Mix gently in rice and cook for
2 minutes:
1 tablespoon butter
In 1/2 cup water, soak:
1 teaspoon saffron leaves or
1/8 teaspoon powdered saffron
When water is bright orange
in color, pour it over the rice
and mix in well. Remove rice
from stove and serve at once,
garnished with:
1 tablespoon blanched chopped
almonds
1 tablespoon white raisins

RED RICE

Melt in frying pan or kettle
with tight cover:
1 tablespoon butter or
margarine
Add:
1 cup dry unwashed rice
Stir rice with wooden spoon
while adding:
1 teaspoon salt
Do not brown rice in fat,
only heat very hot; then
remove from heat and add:
2 cups boiling water
1 teaspoon paprika
2 whole pimientos, diced
Cover at once and return to
heat. Simmer until done. (White
rice, 20 minutes; Texas and
Louisiana brown rice, 30 minutes;
California brown rice, 1 hour.)
Do not remove cover until
done. One cup of rice makes
4 large or 6 small portions.
Serves 6.

GREEN PEPPER RICE

Heat in skillet that can be
tightly covered:
2 tablespoons oil
1 cup unwashed rice
1 teaspoon salt
Mix and add, keeping rice
very hot:
1 teaspoon chopped celery
leaves
1/2 green pepper, cubed
1/4 cup parsley, minced
1/4 cup green onion tops,
chopped
Mix and add:
2 cups boiling water
2 drops green coloring
Cover and simmer 1 hour.

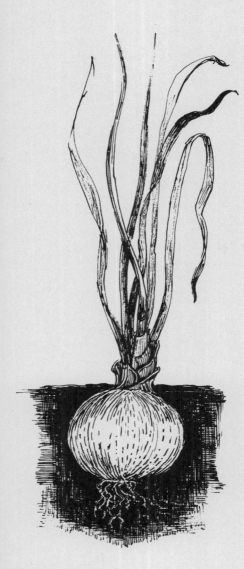

OLIVE CHOW YUK

Cook in the recommended way:
1 cup rice
2 tablespoons butter
1/2 teaspoon salt
Cut into 3/4-inch diagonal
slices:
2 cups celery
Quarter and pull layers apart:
2 medium size onions
Cut into strips:
1 cup green peppers
Mix vegetables and cook for
10 minutes in:
**2 tablespoons olive oil or
cooking oil**
Dissolve in 1 cup hot water:
1/4 teaspoon granulated sugar
1 vegetable cube
Add to vegetables, cover and
cook 10 minutes. Mix together:
**1 tablespoon soya sauce
(page 181)**
1 tablespoon cornstarch
Mix cornstarch and soya with
liquid from vegetables. Add
to vegetables the liquid
mixture and:
3/4 cup chopped ripe olives
(canned broken pieces
can be used)
Serve on hot rice. Serves 4.
This recipe can be changed about
here and there as your
inspiration guides you.

RICE ORIENTAL

Heat in large skillet:
2 tablespoons peanut oil
Add:
2 cups brown rice
Season with:
2 teaspoons salt
1/2 teaspoon turmeric
**1/2 teaspoon powdered cardamon
seed (optional)**
Stir constantly until rice is
browned but not burned;
then remove from flame and
add:
4 cups hot water
4-ounce can diced pimientos
1/2 cup chopped parsley
**1 tablespoon chopped coriander
leaves (optional)**
Cover tightly and steam for
1 hour. Serves 6.

rice and grains

WILD RICE AND MUSHROOMS

When we first opened our dining room to the public in a rather quiet way, I had to invent meatless dishes that would be acceptable to meat eaters, who often came to dine. I hit on the idea of making the broth for wild rice with vegetable cubes, and it worked out very well. The cubes, plus the herbs that I added along with the broth, gave the wild rice a fine flavor.

Wash thoroughly in at least 3 waters, watching for small stones:

1 cup (6 ounces) wild rice

In a large frying pan which can be tightly covered place:

2 tablespoons melted butter

Spread rice in frying pan. Heat, but do not brown the rice, then add:

3 vegetable cubes, dissolved in 3 cups boiling water

1/2 teaspoon herb salt

Cook tightly covered for about 1 hour, or until the rice is tender and swelled up to proper size. Wash and drain in colander:

1 pound fresh mushrooms

Take off stems with a sharp knife and slice into 1/4-inch pieces. Cut caps into 1/6-inch slices, across. Pound in mortar:

1 teaspoon onion salt

2 pinches garlic salt

2 pinches basil

2 pinches thyme

2 pinches rosemary

2 pinches marjoram

2 pinches fresh ground pepper

2 pinches celery seed

Do not omit any of these herbs, for they are balanced in this proportion. Add the herbs to:

1 quart coffee cream

Combine cream and mushrooms in a kettle and heat, but do not boil. Thicken with:

6 tablespoons cornstarch dissolved in a little water

When thick add:

4 tablespoons cream sherry

Serve mushrooms with the wild rice. Serves 8.

WILD RICE
IN CASSEROLE

Boil for 20 minutes and drain:
1 cup wild rice
3 cups water
Melt in pan:
2 tablespoons butter
Add and cook 5 minutes:
1/2 pound chopped mushrooms
1 chopped green pepper
2 chopped onions
Add and cook 10 minutes:
2 cups tomato juice
Then add:
1/2 cup chopped parsley
1/4 teaspoon paprika
1/4 teaspoon thyme
1 teaspoon salt
Have ready:
**3/4 cup grated mild
cheddar cheese**
Place layers of cooked rice,
mushroom mixture and grated
cheese into baking dish and bake
for 45 minutes at 350°.
(Layer it twice). Serves 8.

BROWN RICE PILAU
WITH HERBS

Grind in mortar:
1 teaspoon salt
2 teaspoons onion salt
1/2 teaspoon summer savory
1/2 teaspoon dill seeds
Crush and grind with herbs:
1 clove garlic
Heat over high heat, in pan
with tight cover, until very hot:
2 tablespoons butter
1 cup unwashed, brown rice
Remove from heat and add:
2 cups boiling water
**2 bay leaves (discard when
cooked)**
ground herbs and garlic
Cover tightly and steam on
simmer heat for 1 hour or until
done. (See Red Rice recipe for
cooking time.) The mixture
should have little crater-like
holes in it when it is done.
Serves 6.

SOUTHERN RICE

Melt in frying pan or kettle
with tight cover:
**1 tablespoon butter, margarine
or cooking oil**
Add:
1 cup unwashed rice
Stir with wooden spoon while
adding:
1 teaspoon salt
Do not brown rice in fat but
only get it very hot. Then
remove from heat and add:
2 cups boiling water
Cover at once and return to
heat, simmer until done. (See
Red Rice recipe for cooking
time for different types of
rice.) Serves 6.

rice and grains

CASSEROLE OF THE EAST

Prepare in recommended way:
1 cup brown rice
Mix together:
1/2 cup white sauce
(Bechamel preferred)
1/8 teaspoon curry powder
(Don't make it too strong with curry)
Mix rice and curried sauce together and mound up in a casserole.
Cut in half:
several fresh figs
Lay figs, cut side down, on the mounded rice circular fashion, but do not cover it completely. Sprinkle over the mound:
raw pine nuts, a generous amount.
Put under broiler until pine nuts are slightly brown. This will heat the figs and rice to just the right temperature. Serve immediately. Serves 4.

(This recipe is for one of many delicious dishes served at Gleich's, a fine vegetarian restaurant in Zurich, Switzerland. Manfred Gleich gave it to me especially for this book.)

GREEN RICE

(Preferably prepared in a large stainless steel frying pan.)
Cook slowly until clear:
2 tablespoons oil
1 onion, chopped fine
1 clove garlic, chopped fine
Add and bring to a good boil:
1 4-ounce can green, long chilis,
cut in 1/4-inch pieces (Remove seeds unless hot food is wanted.)
1/2 cup celery leaves,
chopped fine
1/2 cup parsley, chopped fine
1/2 cup fresh French sorrel
leaves (no stems), chopped fine
1/2 cup broccoli leaves,
chopped fine
1/2 cup fresh Swiss chard,
green, chopped fine
2 teaspoons salt
3 cups boiling water
few drops green coloring,
enough to make nice color
Add and stir in after heating very hot:
2 tablespoons butter
2 cups dry white rice
Cover pan tightly and cook until done. (See Red Rice recipe for cooking time for different types of rice.)
Serves 6.

entrees

ENTREES

If you are one of the many people now beginning a meatless diet, you may feel that one of your biggest problems is what to prepare for an entree. Other parts of the meal are simple but: "All I know how to fix is macaroni and cheese!"

The change to a vegetarian diet will be easier and more fun if you start with a wholly new approach to eating, free of worry about substituting one thing for another. So many of the suggested 'vegi' substitutes for meat are very dull, and eating things that don't start the digestive juices flowing will not create the proper digestive climate. I have tried to invent things that will inspire the appetite and please the palate.

Again I say, don't look for substitutes. There aren't any, really, although there are some so-called meat substitutes that are tasty and nutritionally valuable. Old habits may linger for awhile, perhaps some cravings will plague you, but you have a new world of food to think about and if you ignore the old ways they will quickly fade. In deciding to change your eating habits you are probably beginning to listen to your own body wisdom. Just eat things that for you combine happily for texture and flavor—and enjoy your meal!

Of course there are dietary considerations, but no great complications. Common sense will safely guide you. Protein is necessary in the diet but perhaps not as much as we have assumed. It is said that too much protein produces an oversupply of uric acid, thus working the kidneys too hard. I have tried to put most of these entrees together so that dietary requirements will not be neglected. Some of the dishes are higher in protein and in minerals and vitamins than meat. Many types of nuts, seeds, cheese, grains and milk products are used. Soya protein is said to be superior even to meat. The

entrees

easiest way to get this protein is in soya flour which can be added to many things. Avoid overuse of the many processed foods such as sugars, starches and fats. If you drink coffee or tea, be sure to get plenty of the vitamin B complex in your diet; this seems to be helpful in preventing the nervousness caffeine can cause. These stimulants are said to burn up the blood sugar and in the process use up the B vitamins.

Many books on nutrition and dieting say you must eat meat; just as many books say eating meat is a terrible dietary error. I say why not experiment and enjoy the experience of something different. For awhile try one diet that appeals to you, then try another; then go with the one that provides you with the most energy and harmony of spirit.

Here are some suggestions that may be useful:

Try starting your meal with fresh raw fruit—an apple or an orange, a peach or pear, grapes or a melon. Or with raw vegetables, perhaps in a salad. Hard to chew vegetables like carrots, celery, cabbage and beets can be put through the gricer. Use an easily prepared dressing of oil and vinegar, or a simple French dressing. Eat small amounts, chewing everything well. The most wonderful flavors will be your rich reward.

Don't bother to think in terms of an entree—prepare what you feel you would like to eat. Let your natural food wants, those the body will project, come to the surface. Perhaps to your surprise, this approach will result in a delicious and satisfying meal.

If you will pay attention to its messages your body will guide you. Become aware—listen carefully with great confidence! Experiment! Experiment!

Experiment! If you choose wrongly now and then, what does it matter—you have found out something. Either you didn't like the taste of that dish or it was not suitable for you at the time you ate it. There are no mistakes, you are learning a completely different way of nourishing yourself. Don't depend on an outside authority. It's your body, unlike any other body. It is your problem to nourish it and enjoy the process. Your meat eating friends will have things to say, such as: "Do you think you are getting enough protein?" or "Will all that raw stuff agree with you?" And, most tiresomely, you'll get 'recommended' diets. Don't waste time giving logical explanations. Just tell them you're having fun trying something new.

Sometimes people get sick, and eventually we all die—what of it! For the time being we are alive—so be it!

STUFFED ARTICHOKES

With scissors clip the tops from
4 large artichokes
Cut off the stems and, with a
melon ball maker scoop out the
"chokes." Only cut down to the
bottom of the artichoke; do not
cut into it. Cook artichokes and
stems in pressure cooker at
15 pounds pressure for 10 minutes
with 1/4 cup water. When cool
enough to handle spread apart
the leaves slightly so the
stuffing can be easily put in
the center hole. To make
stuffing, braise until clear:
2 tablespoons butter
2 green onions including tops,
chopped fine
Add and cook for 2 minutes more:

1 cup mushrooms, chopped fine
Add and mix well:
1 cup shredded mild cheddar
cheese
1/2 cup bread crumbs
1/2 teaspoon salt
1/8 teaspoon chervil
good dash black pepper
Mix together and add:
2 eggs well beaten
1/2 cup sour cream
Stuff the artichokes with this
mixture. Remove skin from stems
if it is tough. Chop stems and
put on top of stuffing. Add some
grated cheese.
Bake at 400° for 30 minutes.
Serve with small dish of
drawn butter
for dipping artichoke leaves.
Serves 4.

entrees

FRIENDS IN NEED

When we were in the process of building the new Ranch House and getting ready to serve the public, we needed help and enlisted the aid of two very good friends, Fred and Torre Taggart.

When we finally opened the restaurant and started serving, Fred made the whole wheat and date-nut bread, struggling with an old broken-down oven that we bought for little money, and that never did work properly. Torre cooked and served with my help. In my opinion she is one of the best and most creative cooks I know. She left us a group of wonderful dishes, one of which is given here.

In the restaurant, I take credit for these things, though of course if you ask I will have to say the name of the originator.

EGGPLANT ROMA

Slice in pieces 1/2 inch thick:
2 eggplants, unpeeled
Broil the slices quickly as possible on both sides, and put them at once in a crockery or glass baking dish. Add lightly:
salt
On each slice of eggplant, place a slice of:
Provolone cheese, about half the size of the eggplant slices.
Sprinkle over them lightly:
Bakon yeast (optional)
Spoon over slices, without disturbing the yeast:
Italian sauce (page 16)
Do not use too much cheese and tomato sauce. There should be two, or perhaps three, layers, depending on the size of the baking dish. Bake at 350° for about 30 minutes until the sauce begins to bubble gently around the edges. Over-baking will toughen the cheese and over-cook the sauce and eggplant. Serves 8.
Serve with saffron rice (page 141), a perfect accompaniment for this eggplant dish.

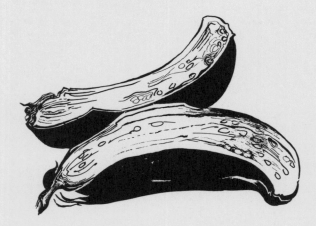

EGGPLANT A L'ALGERIENNE

Saute in butter, lightly;
8 large mushrooms, sliced
1 shallot, or
1 tablespoon onion, chopped
1 tablespoon flour
When done, blend in:
1/2 cup light cream
Reduce liquid a little by
simmering.
(Any good mushroom sauce will
do if the above is not suitable).

Cut 1/2 inch thick:
8 slices eggplant
Either dip slices in cream then
flour and fry in fat until
golden brown, or brown under
broiler without any further
preparation.
Cut:
8 slices tomato, 3/4 inch thick
Dip tomato slices in flour
only, and fry.

Spread over bottom of shallow,
long baking dish:
1 cup cooked rice pilau (page 99)
Alternate and overlap edges of
eggplant slices and tomato
slices. Pour mushroom sauce over
this. Bake at 350° until
mixture begins to bubble. Do
not overcook or eggplant and
tomatoes will turn to mush.
Serves 8.

STUFFED EGGPLANT

Cut 1 inch off from top of
eggplant and set aside for use
later.
Hollow out, leaving sides about
1/2 inch thick:
4 eggplants
Put in large kettle with about
1 inch of water and steam for
9 minutes. Remove and allow
to cool.

Mix together for stuffing:
1 cup cooked rice
1/4 cup raw minced onion
1/2 cup braised mushrooms
3/4 cup shredded cheddar cheese
2 eggs, unbeaten
1/4 cup bread crumbs
**1 teaspoon fresh basil leaves,
crushed (dried ones will do)**
1/2 teaspoon herb salt
**2 tablespoons chopped green
peppers**
2 tablespoons olive oil
Stuff the eggplants with this
mixture. Put on the caps which
were laid aside. Bake at 400°
for about 1-1/2 to 2 hours.
Slice them in half horizontally.
Lift off top half with spatula
and invert it to serve, thus
making 2 servings of each
eggplant. Spoon over each
portion a very light cheese
sauce. Serves 8.

entrees

BROCCOLI WITH SAUCE

Heat in small sauce pan:
2 cups buttermilk
1 cup yogurt
4 tablespoons cornstarch
Grind in mortar:
1/2 teaspoon onion salt
1/4 teaspoon garlic salt
dash MSG (optional)
dash winter savory
Add:
1 teaspoon capers
1 teaspoon turmeric
Grind together and add to
buttermilk mixture. Then heat
gently until it thickens.
Add to mixture to smooth it out:
4 tablespoons sour cream
Wash thoroughly, cook and drain:
2-1/2 pounds fresh broccoli
enough for 6 sizable servings
Put 1/2 cup water into pressure
cooker. Lay in broccoli and put
on cover. Heat until steam has
been escaping for 1/2 minute.
Put on pressure gauge and when
pressure is correct, cook just
1/2 minute, then cool pressure
cooker immediately under
running cold water. Remove
lid immediately and allow steam
to escape. Replace lid to await
serving. To serve, place cooked
broccoli on plate and gently
spoon sauce over it, not adding
too much. Serves 6.

AVOCADO LOAF

Mix well together:
1 egg, well beaten
1 pound ground vegeburger
2 tablespoons onion, minced fine
2 tablespoons celery tops,
chopped fine
4 tablespoons catsup
1-1/2 teaspoon salt
1 cup soft bread crumbs
1 avocado, peeled and mashed,
but not too fine
2 tablespoons parsley, chopped
This amount will just fill a
12-hole muffin tin, well greased.
Bake in very hot oven, 400° for
20 minutes. Do not overcook, as
an acid taste will develop from
the avocado.

To prepare sauce for this dish,
cook clear:
1 tablespoon onion, minced
1 tablespoon butter
Brown in dry pan, stirring
constantly:
4 tablespoons ordinary white
flour. Do not allow it to
get too brown or scorch.

Add and mix well, then cool:
2 tablespoons butter
Add and mix well, then cook
until thickened:
cleared onions
1 cup water
1 vegetable cube
1 tablespoon shreddded cheddar
cheese
dash fresh ground pepper
1/2 teaspoon Worcestershire
sauce
few drops lime or lemon juice
Add after gravy has thickened:
1/2 avocado, peeled and
mashed, but not too fine
Sauce should be brown in color if
flour was browned properly.
A small amount of chopped parsley
may be added if desired. Do not
overheat after adding avocado,
or an acid taste will develop.
Serves 6.

STUFFED YELLOW SQUASH

Trim and cut in half:
**18 medium size yellow
crookneck squash**
Scoop out centers with melon
ball maker or small spoon.

Cook clear:
**2 tablespoons butter
4 cups minced onion
1 clove garlic
1 teaspoon herb salt**
Add and cook until just
tender, not soft:
**squash centers
2 large sprigs winter savory
2 large sprigs fresh basil
1/4 cup chopped parsley
2 vegetable cubes**
Mix into the above:
**1 cup chopped English walnuts
1/2 cup bread crumbs
1/2 cup wheat germ
2 eggs
2 tablespoons grated cheese**
Steam squash halves until just
tender, not soft, and place in
flat baking pan. Spoon in filling
and bake at 375° for
30 minutes. Serves 6.

CHOP SUEY
AND SAUCE

Prepare and mix together:
**8 stalks celery, sliced
thin diagonally
2 onions, sliced thin
1/2 green pepper, sliced thin
4 water chestnuts, sliced thin
8 tablespoons bamboo shoots,
sliced thin
4 tablespoons whole blanched
almonds
2 cups bean sprouts, whole**
Put into kettle with tight
lid and get very hot:
4 tablespoons peanut oil
Add vegetables and:
1/2 cup hot water
Steam until just done and
still crisp.

Into 4 cups water add:
**6 slices choplets, cut in long
thin pieces
1/2 teaspoon MSG (optional)
3 tablespoons soya sauce
2 tablespoons savita
1/2 cup dry or fresh
mushrooms, cut up**
Thicken with:
cornstarch dissolved in cold water
Add sauce to vegetables and
serve hot. Serves 8.

TOMATO AND CELERY CASSEROLE

Cut off and reserve tops of:
3 cups celery, cut into 1-inch pieces
Add:
1/2 teaspoon herb salt
Steam in very little water until celery is just soft. Cut into 1-inch cubes and spread over celery:
8 slices white or whole wheat bread, lightly buttered.
Spread in a thick layer over the bread:
2 cups sharp cheddar cheese, grated
Drain and press seeds from:
1 No. 2-1/2 can Italian tomatoes, the long, meaty variety.
(Reserve the juice for soup stock.) Lay these flattened tomatoes over the cheese; there should be enough to cover it but if not, another small can also should be used.

Mix together:
6 tablespoons coffee cream
6 tablespoons white flour
Add:
6 eggs, well beaten
1/2 teaspoon herb salt
1/2 teaspoon oregano, pulverized
1/2 teaspoon basil
Add mixture to casserole, pressing down a little so it will penetrate well into the layers. Chop fine and spread over casserole mixture:
celery tops
Bake at 400° for 45 minutes, or until egg custard is set but not dry. Cut in squares and serve, garnished with chopped parsley. Serves 6.

GREEN BEAN STEW— PENNSYLVANIA

This is an excellent dish which, on first reading, may seem a bit too complicated but actually isn't. The potatoes, vegetables and beans are cooked separately, then the gravy is made from the bean juice and all ingredients added and reheated—that is the simple way of it.

Prepare by cooking with skins on, then peeling and cutting into eighths:
6 medium sized potatoes
Cook 5 minutes in pressure cooker, without cap:

2 tablespoons butter
1 large onion, finely chopped
3 stalks celery, cut in 1-inch pieces
Grind in mortar:
1 tablespoon herb salt
1/4 teaspoon summer savory (very important)
1/4 teaspoon thyme
Add:
2 tablespoons Bakon yeast, mixed with
1 teaspoon salt
Put in pressure cooker, adding the herb mixture, and cook 1-1/2 minutes at 15 pounds:
1-1/2 pounds fresh green beans, cut in pieces
1/2 cup water
Drain liquid from beans, adding water to make 1-1/2 cups, and thicken with:
4 tablespoons flour, well blended in
4 tablespoons butter
Combine all ingredients and add:
1 small can diced pimientos
1 bay leaf (discard when cooked)
1 can choplets, cut into 1 x 1/2-inch pieces
Heat to serving temperature and let stand for at least 30 minutes. Serves 6.

entrees

SAUERKRAUT AND CHOPLETS

Drain and spread around evenly in large frying pan:

1 large can sauerkraut

(The above can be done after the choplets are fried, using same pan.) Melt in frying pan:

1/2 cup butter (1 stick)

When thoroughly melted add:

2 tablespoons Bakon yeast

Fry in this mixture until brown on both sides:

1 large can choplets, well drained (save juice)

The choplets will stick and will have to be loosened with a pancake turner or spatula, but this brown crust has the flavor of the yeast, which is important. When brown, lay the choplets on top of the sauerkraut, adding the brown parts that have come loose in the frying process, along with any butter that has not been absorbed.

Add on top of choplets:

2 tablespoons onion, minced fine

Add:

juice from choplet can

Cover and steam slowly for 30 minutes. Serve with applesauce which has been prepared as follows:

Mix thoroughly and let stand for at least 30 minutes:

1 quart applesauce, fresh or canned
1 tablespoon creme de menthe
1 teaspoon cardamon seed, powdered

Serves 8.

TAMALE PIE

Fry slowly for 15 minutes:

2 chopped onions
2 cloves garlic, chopped
1/3 cup olive oil

Add:

1 chopped green pepper
1 No. 2-1/2 can tomatoes

10 ounces corn kernels
2 tablespoons chili powder
1 small can vegeburger

Grind in mortar, add to above and cook 15 minutes:

1 teaspoon salt
1/2 teaspoon MSG (optional)
1 large sprig oregano (1/4 teaspoon)
1 large sprig thyme (1/4 teaspoon)
1 large sprig basil (1/4 teaspoon)

In separate pan, cook until thick:

3 cups milk
1 cup yellow cornmeal

Add and stir well:

3 beaten eggs

Mix all ingredients and add:

1 cup pitted ripe olives

Bake one hour at 350°, then add:

1/2 pound shredded cheddar cheese

sprinkled over top. Return to oven and bake 10 minutes. Serves 8.

QUICK CURRY

Cook until clear:
1 large onion, minced
2 cloves garlic, minced
2 tablespoons butter
Add and simmer 5 minutes or
until a thick paste is formed:
2 tablespoons curry powder
Add and simmer 30 minutes
(All vegetables precooked):
1 cup water
4 vegetable cubes
1 cup lima beans
1 cup cut-up zucchini
1 cup string beans
1 cup onions, cut coarse
1 cup celery, cut coarse
1/2 cup braised mushrooms
Then add: 1 cup peas, uncooked
Blend all ingredients with:
1/2 cup sour cream
For flavoring add:
6 tablespoons jam or marmalade
1/4 cup lemon juice
Adjust seasoning with salt.
Serve with rice. Serves 8.

VEGETARIAN GUMBO

Cook until just tender, about
15 minutes:
1 cup water
1-1/2 cups celery, cut coarse
1 cup onions, cut coarse
1/4 cup chopped parsley
1/2 teaspoon salt
1/4 teaspoon paprika
4 vegetable cubes
1 tablespoon sugar
1/4 teaspoon MSG (optional)
4 bay leaves (discard)
1/4 teaspoon ground pepper
2 tablespoons butter
1 small can vegetable
choplets (optional)
Add and boil 5 minutes:
1/2 No. 2-1/2 can tomatoes,
mashed
Thicken with:
2-1/2 tablespoons cornstarch,
dissolved in a little water
Add and heat to boiling but do
not boil:
2 cups cooked okra
Sprinkle in hot mixture, dry,
and stir in immediately:
1 tablespoon gumbo filet
Heat again without boiling, and
serve with rice. Serves 8.

FRESH CORN CASSEROLE

Warm in large kettle:
1 quart milk
1-1/2 pounds frozen corn niblets
2 teaspoons white sugar
1-1/2 tablespoons butter
Grind in mortar and add:
1/4 teaspoon MSG (optional)
1 teaspoon salt
1/4 teaspoon thyme
1/4 teaspoon marjoram
1/4 teaspoon basil
1/8 teaspoon black pepper
Then add:
5 slightly beaten eggs
Chop fine and add:
1/2 green pepper
2 pimientos
1/4 cup parsley
1 green onion
Bake in buttered casserole
placed in hot water for
1-1/4 hours at 325°. Serves 8.

entrees

FRESH MUSHROOM AND CHESTNUT LOAF

Mix well together and put into greased baking pan:

1 large onion, chopped fine
(1-1/2 cups)
1 cup celery, chopped fine
and braised in butter
1/2 cup chopped parsley
1/4 pound ground walnuts
1/2 cup wheat germ
1 cup old-fashioned oatmeal
5 slices dry bread, made into
crumbs
1-1/4 pounds chestnuts, roasted,
peeled and cut coarse
1/4 pound mushrooms, chopped
and braised in butter
1 can vegetable burger (optional,
but necessary for best results)
6 eggs

Mix together, heat but do not boil, and add:

3/4 cup milk
3 vegetable cubes
1 teaspoon salt
1/4 teaspoon herb blend
1 pinch powdered sage

Bake 1 hour at 400°. Serves 8.

PECAN LOAF

Mix well together:

1-1/2 cups celery, cut fine
1-1/2 cups whole wheat bread
crumbs
(If a milder taste is wanted,
use white bread crumbs)
1-1/2 cups ground pecan meats
3 tablespoons onion, chopped
very fine
2-1/2 cups milk
3 tablespoons chopped parsley
1 teaspoon herb salt
3 well-beaten eggs
3 tablespoons melted butter

Let stand for 20 minutes then bake in buttered loaf pan at 375° for 45 to 50 minutes until nicely browned. Make a sauce, using:

4 tablespoons flour
4 tablespoons butter

Add and cook until thickened, stirring constantly:

2 cups milk, mixed with
1 egg yolk
1/2 cup parsley, minced
dash white pepper
1/2 bay leaf

When thick, remove bay leaf *immediately.* Spoon over servings of loaf, generously. Serves 8.

ESSIE'S CHESTNUT CASSEROLE

Slit each nutshell; roast for 20 minutes:

1 pound Italian chestnuts

Cool enough to handle, remove outside husk and inside skin, then slice very thin. Lay one-third of sliced chestnuts in well-buttered casserole with:

2 large onions, sliced thin
(use 1/2-inch layer)

Add a layer of:

sharp cheddar cheese, shredded

Continue the layers in this order, with the last one-third of the chestnuts on the top. Pour over layers:

1 small can evaporated milk.

Bake at 375° for 45 minutes. Make sauce by mixing together:

1 cup sliced mushrooms
2 green onions, chopped fine
4 tablespoons butter
1/4 teaspoon herb salt

Cook until done, then add and stir in well:

2 cups sour cream

Heat to serving temperature and spoon over chestnut loaf portions on plate. Garnish with:

minced parsley and
paprika. Serves 6.

NUT LOAF

Braise very lightly:
4 tablespoons butter
3 cups chopped celery
Mix well together, then
combine with celery:
3 cups finely chopped onions
1 cup almonds, ground into
flour in blender
2 cups chopped walnuts
2 cups toasted cashews, chopped
1/2 cup rolled oats
1/4 cup sesame meal
1/4 cup sunflower seeds
2 pounds cottage cheese
1/4 can vegeburger
or 1 cup cooked rice
4 teaspoons salt
1/4 teaspoon black pepper
1/2 teaspoon herb blend
6 eggs
Bake in greased loaf pans for at
least 1 hour, at 400°. Bake
an additional 1/2 hour if firmer
loaf is desired. Serves 8.

NUT AND LENTIL LOAF

Soak overnight then cook in
pressure cooker for 20 minutes
at 15 pounds:
2 cups lentils
4 cups water
Mix together and cook over low
heat for 15 minutes:
4 tablespoons butter
4 tablespoons Bakon yeast
mixed in a little water
12 stalks celery, minced fine
4 cloves garlic, minced fine
1 teaspoon savory herb blend
1 teaspoon herb salt
4 teaspoons salt
Mix lentils and celery mixture
together and add:
4 cups onions, minced fine
4 eggs
1 cup old-fashioned rolled oats
1 cup walnuts, broken up but
not too fine
1 cup raw almonds (unblanched),
chopped coarse
Mix well together and shape
into two loaves. Bake in
well-buttered breadpans at 400°
for at least 1 hour. To make
gravy for this loaf, mix
together and cook very slowly
for 1/2 hour:
4 tablespoons butter
2 cups onions, minced
1 vegetable cube
Mix together, add to cooked
onions and cook until thickened:
2 tablespoons flour
4 tablespoons Gravy Quick or
enough savita for desired flavor
3 cups water
2 tablespoons cornstarch,
dissolved in a little of the
water.
When thickened add:
2 tablespoons tomato catsup
This loaf can be cut into
portions when cold and frozen
for future use. Wrap each
portion in foil then put the
wrapped slices in a plastic bag
for freezing. Defrost the number
of slices you need. Put about
4 tablespoons of water in a
small skillet and lay the
foil-wrapped slices in it, being
careful that no water gets into
the packages. Cover tightly
and steam for about 3 minutes.

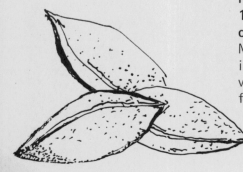

WALNUT CROQUETS

Grind in blender:
2 cups walnuts
Mix together, adding ground walnuts:
1/2 cup sesame seeds, raw
1/2 cup wheat germ
1/2 cup grated cheddar cheese
4 green onions and tops, chopped fine
1/4 cup chopped parsley
2 eggs
1 teaspoon savita, dissolved in 1 tablespoon hot water
1 pinch savory, powdered
1/2 teaspoon salt
Form mixture into patties and fry slowly until brown in:
butter
Serve with cheese sauce or tomato sauce. Serves 6.

ALMOND CROQUETS

Grind in blender:
2 cups raw, unblanched almonds
Mix together, adding almond meal, then make into cutlets:
1/2 cup wheat germ
1/2 cup raw sesame seeds
1 small onion, minced, or
4 green onions and tops, minced
1 clove garlic, minced
8 ounces cottage cheese
2 eggs
1 teaspoon savita, dissolved in
1 tablespoon hot water
1 pinch curry powder
1 teaspoon salt
Fry slowly until brown in:
butter
Do not fry quickly, as they will burn and not be done through. They should be crisp on the outside. Serve with cheese sauce or tomato sauce. Serves 6.

CASHEW CALAVO

Mix well together:
1 cup whole cashews, unsalted, raw
1 cup pignolia nuts, unsalted, raw
1 cup cooked rice—turmeric or plain
1 cup Bechamel or rich cream sauce.
Mound this mixture on:
6 avocado halves, peeled
Put in shallow baking dish close together, or in individual baking dishes. Spoon over each half:
Mornay or any rich cheese sauce.
Bake until sauce begins to bubble. Serve very hot. Serves 6.

entrees

BROILED MUSHROOMS

I had an amusing experience on my first visit to the famous Antoine's in New Orleans, and the thing I remember most vividly is a dish of mushrooms. We asked the waiter about the various vegetarian dishes available and discussed each one—the sauces used, and so forth. Finally, we ordered a fairly simple meal. The waiter misunderstood, either deliberately or because he did not know English very well. Lo and behold! Two waiters began bringing in trays piled with dishes, enough to fill our large table and the one next to it!

After the first shock, I was delighted at this opportunity to sample such a variety of foods! Of all this largess, the dish that remains most clearly in my memory is a particular type of broiled mushrooms, as much as three inches in diameter, thick as a steak and dark in color. When you cut them, they were solid without being tough. I think they must have been broiled in butter, then turned

116

upside down and the cap filled with a mixture of onion, garlic, Worcestershire and a bit of thyme. This flavor had permeated the mushrooms, making them absolutely divine.

Here is the way we serve them at the Ranch House. Use quantities of mushrooms and toast sufficient for the number of servings you need. Prepare:
well-buttered toast,
not too dry and crisp, with just a suggestion of:
garlic in the butter
mushrooms
the largest you can find; the brown (russet) type if available. The russet mushrooms have the most flavor and do not shrink in the cooking as much as other mushrooms do. The 'skirt' should be tightly attached to the stem, for then they are freshly picked and not dry. Wash them well under running water and scrub off any bits of dirt imbedded in the top or at the end of the stem. Do not peel them. Cut the stem off even with the bottom part of the mushroom; do not break it off for then a hole is left in the under side of

the mushroom.
In a frying pan melt a generous amount of:
sweet butter
Lay the mushrooms in the pan cut side down. Cover and cook slowly until they feel as soft as the side of the forearm. Covering the pan is essential to keep the mushrooms from drying out. When done on the first side, turn them with tongs. Put onto each stem:
Worcestershire sauce, 2 or
3 drops
herb salt, a good dash
Continue cooking under cover until the second side is gently brown. Have ready a hot platter with the hot toast on it. Lift out the mushrooms without spilling any of the delicious juice in the cap. Turn them over on the toast so the liquor will soak into it. Any liquor left in the pan should be spooned over each serving. These mushrooms make a delicious accompaniment to scrambled eggs, or served with green cooked vegetables or a salad. Surprisingly, they are enough, with any of the above suggestions, to create a satisfying meal.

EGG AND MUSHROOM CUTLETS

Saute:
4 tablespoons butter
1/2 teaspoon herb salt
2 cups fresh mushrooms, sliced
1 green onion, minced
Make a roux with:
3 tablespoons butter
3 tablespoons flour
Add and cook until thick:
1 cup milk
1/2 teaspoon salt
2 teaspoons minced parsley
Hardboil:
6 eggs
Cool eggs, separate yolks from whites, then rub through sieve, reserving a little of the sieved whites for garnishing.

Mix mushrooms, white sauce and eggs together and add:
bread crumbs, enough to make a dough.
Spread dough on platter and when cool form into cutlets. Dip into:
beaten egg
then into:
bread crumbs
and fry in butter until nicely browned. Serves 6.

entrees

PERUSKA PERIOG
(A Real Russian Dish)

Mix together as for pie dough:
1 cup white pie flour
6 tablespoons butter (3/4 stick)
1 teaspoon salt
Make a well in the flour mixture and add:
1/3 cup buttermilk
Mix until dough will just hold together. Roll out thin and line an 8 x 8 x 1-1/2-inch baking dish. Reserve a little less than half of the dough for the top crust.
For the filling, mix together and cook until soft but not mushy:
2 tablespoons butter
1/2 onion, sliced thin
1 cup mushrooms, sliced thin
1 cup cabbage, cut into half-inch squares
1/2 teaspoon omelette herb blend, ground with:
3/4 teaspoon herb salt
Combine and stir gently into cooked mixture:
4 hard boiled eggs, sliced
3/4 cup rich cream sauce
Spread mixture in dough-lined baking dish and dot with:
sweet butter
Roll out top crust and put it
118

on, pressing down the edges. Make a few slits for steam to escape. Bake at 450° for about 25 minutes or until crust is light brown and crisp; it needs cooking only until the crust is done. Cut in squares and serve immediately. Serves 6.

CURRIED MUSHROOMS AND EGGS

Cook clear and to a paste:
2 tablespoons butter
1 clove garlic, chopped fine
2 onions, chopped fine
Add and simmer gently 20 minutes:
1-1/2 tablespoon curry powder
Braise in butter:
2 cups fresh mushrooms, sliced
Add to above and bring to gentle bubbling:
2 small cans mushroom soup
2 ounces milk
Add:
3 tablespoons jelly or marmalade
2 tablespoons lemon juice
1/2 cup peas (optional)
Hard boil and peel:
4 eggs, cut into eighths
Slice eggs in dish and spoon curry over them. Serves 4.

FRESH MUSHROOM CUTLETS

These are easy to make but must be made at the very last moment before frying them:
1 cup mushroom stems and pieces, chopped fine
1 green onion, chopped fine
Beat together; mix with mushrooms and onion:
2 eggs
1/2 teaspoon herb salt
Add and stir in well but do not make a soft mush:
1/2 cup bread crumbs
3/4 cup grated cheddar cheese, mild
Divide into 8 patties about 3/4 inch thick and press into shape between folds of waxed paper. Fry in butter, not too hot. The outside of the cutlet should be crisp and the inside moist. Serve with
Mornay sauce.
Serves 4.

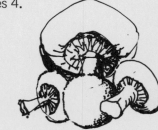

CHEESE

*"Milk's leap toward
immortality."* —*Clifton Fadiman*

If you are going to melt cheese
into a sauce or fondue, keep in
mind that new, green cheese
will not melt but turns into a
sort of gum. In fact, it is
well to remember that all
protein, unless somehow
modified, will curdle, thicken
or become rubbery when heated.
Eggs, cheese and wheat gluten
get leathery; milk will curdle
at the least error.

In cheese, the process of aging
somehow affects the cheese so
that it will melt; therefore,
cheese for dishes such as
Welsh Rarebit should always be
aged. A simple way to tell
whether or not cheese is aged
is to break it. Aged cheese
will crumble easily; green
cheese will not. It takes at
least a year to age good cheese
properly. I think none of the
so-called "processed" cheeses
will satisfy those who
appreciate natural cheese, nor
will processing ever take the
place of natural aging in
cheese.

119

entrees

GREEN ONION AND CHEESE CASSEROLE

Braise until just done:
1 bunch green onions, tops included, chopped
4 tablespoons butter
1/4 cup sunflower seeds, hulled
Beat together and then mix with cooked onions:
4 eggs
1-1/2 cups milk
8 ounces Philadelphia cream cheese, crumbled
1/4 teaspoon herb salt
1 tablespoon minced parsley
Butter and then cube:
2 slices white bread
Lay bread cubes in buttered casserole. Pour onion and egg mixture over them. Bake at 375° for about 25 minutes or until knife blade comes out clean. Serve immediately without sauce or garnish. Serves 4.
This is a subtly flavored dish; people who like strongly-flavored food may find it too bland.

WELSH RAREBIT

Don't be put off if it's called Welsh Rabbit—it is all the same dish! The important thing is to use a well-aged cheese. Cheddar is used most often but other varieties such as Swiss and Gruyere are also used.
I shall always remember having Welsh Rarebit late at night in the basement dining room of the old Deshler-Wallick hotel in Columbus, Ohio. I think it was the best rarebit I ever had, and always when I make it this remembered taste is what I try to recreate; imitate, even, if you wish—for I don't feel guilty about trying to imitate a dish I have especially enjoyed. It is a lot of fun, if you are interested in cooking, to try duplicating what you have liked. Here is a recipe especially liked by many people—very rich and heavy when not diluted with cream or any other sauce. You can dilute if you wish—I will take it straight, served on toast and very hot. It must be heated slowly to keep it smooth and free from roughness in texture.

Put into double boiler:
8 ounces cheddar cheese, grated
2 tablespoons butter—sweet butter is better
1/4 cup stale beer (English ale, if possible)
1/4 cup cream (optional) or
1/4 cup Bechamel Sauce (optional)
When mixture is melted to a smooth consistency, beat in:
1 egg
Then add for seasoning:
1/4 teaspoon Worcestershire sauce
1/4 teaspoon paprika
dash cayenne
1/4 teaspoon dry mustard (optional)
Serve over toast. If using small casseroles, put under the broiler for a moment to make sure it will be piping hot. It can also be served fondue-style in a chafing dish or kept warm on an electric tray and served with long strips of toast, to be used for dipping.

CHEESE FONDUE, AMERICAN STYLE

Scald:
2 cups milk
Add and mix well together:
1/2 pound grated sharp cheddar cheese
4 cups soft bread crumbs, chopped fine
1 tablespoon butter
When mixture is cool, add and fold in well:
9 egg yolks, well beaten
1/2 teaspoon salt
Beat well:
9 egg whites
1/2 teaspoon salt
Fold whites into mixture, one-half at a time. Bake at 350° for about 30 minutes. Spoon over servings:
light cheese sauce or white sauce, with plenty of chopped parsley added.
Serves 6.

SWISS FONDUE

Use a pyrex or other baking dish that will withstand direct heat. Rub the inside with garlic. Pour into baking dish:
1-1/2 cups dry white wine
Add and mix well:
1 pound well-aged Swiss cheese, grated (Be sure cheese is well-aged, or it will toughen into rubber!)
Stir constantly over low heat until cheese is melted. This may look hopeless at first but persist—it will come out partly thick and partly thin.
Thicken with:
3 tablespoons potato starch dissolved in
3 tablespoons cold water
When thick, add and stir well:
2 tablespoons Kirsch (imported Swiss)
dash nutmeg (optional)

Serve in heated casserole or chafing dish, with pieces of French sour dough bread, to be dipped in it. Very good for a party, especially if accompanied by a good beer. Serves 6.

entrees

SWISS CHEESE PIE

Saute but do not brown:
4 tablespoons butter
1 bunch green onions, tops
included, chopped
Make a pie dough and line
baking dish, or use:
33 soda crackers,
rolled into crumbs and mixed
with
6 tablespoons melted butter
Spread cooked onions in baking
dish, then mix well and pour
over them:
2 eggs
3/4 cup sour cream
2-1/2 cups grated Swiss cheese
1/2 teaspoon salt
dash white pepper or cayenne
Bake at 350° for
40 minutes or until a knife
comes out clean. Serves 6.

CHEESE BLINTZES

To make the crepes, place in
electric mixer:
1 egg
5 tablespoons milk
5 tablespoons water
pinch salt
Milk should be refrigerator
temperature and water cold from
tap. This is important, as a
warm mix tends to fry too
quickly and stick to the pan.
Mix well.
Sift in; then beat at high
speed for at least 5 minutes:
1/3 cup flour
Allow to stand for at least
1 hour so froth will settle.
Keep cool.
Use a 7-inch frying pan, shiny
clean. Using a pastry brush,
grease pan and allow to get
very hot—grease should be slightly
smoking. Pick up pan and spoon
into it a large cooking spoon
full of batter, rolling the pan
around quickly so as to cover
the bottom with batter. Replace
pan on heat for 45 seconds.
Take off stove and turn pan
upside down on greased board to
release pancake. Be sure batter
is well stirred before each
spoonful is taken out, to keep
flour from settling.
To make filling for blintzes,
beat thoroughly:
1 cup hoop cheese (soft
baker's cheese)
1 egg
Add:
2 teaspoons lemon juice
2 teaspoons pineapple juice
1 tablespoon sugar
pinch salt
dash cinnamon
dash cardamon

Beat well again.
Put a large cooking spoonful
of mixture on the brown side of
each crepe, turn edges over it
and roll crepe into a long
cylinder. Butter one side and
cook slowly on grill until
brown; butter other side and
turn over and cook until brown.
Serve 3 to each person.

QUICHE LORRAINE

Slice thin and fry until
cleared:
**2-1/2 cups sliced onions, in
2 tablespoons butter**
Roll into crumbs, rather fine:
33 soda crackers, salted variety
Melt and mix with crumbs:
6 tablespoons butter
Line a deep, 9-inch pie pan with
the buttered crumbs and spread
onions in it.
Scald, then remove from heat:
1-1/2 cups milk
Add:
**1/2 pound sharp cheddar cheese,
shredded.** (This melts and
cools milk so eggs will not
curdle.)
Mix cheese and milk, then add:
3 beaten eggs
1 teaspoon salt
**1/4 teaspoon black pepper,
fresh ground**
1 teaspoon Worcestershire sauce
Stir well and pour over cooked
onions in pie pan. Bake at 350°
for 40 minutes. Serves 6.
One of the beautiful things
about Quiche Lorraine is that
the recipe can be varied in many
ways. One variation is to

prepare 1/2 cup of lightly
browned natural almonds (those
with the skin left on), very
lightly salted with herb salt
and buttered. Spread these on
the crust before adding the
other ingredients. Yet another
variation is to add a teaspoon
of Bakon yeast to the almonds.
Other nuts may be used—lightly
toasted of course. (This also
keeps them from getting soggy.)
Try chopped cashews or pecans,
or pine nuts, to add flavor
and texture.

Another variation is to saute
in butter 1 cup mushrooms,
sliced very thin and lightly
salted, and spread them on the
crust first. Be sure the
mushrooms are sliced thin so
they won't tear up the filling
when served. In place of
mushrooms you can use zucchini,
pieces of cooked eggplant or
green peppers, or a combination
of vegetables. Remember that
some of the vegetables will
need to be cooked before using.

Eggs are the integral part of
the liquid but cream can be

used instead of milk, or you
can use vegetable juices such
as tomato, celery or carrot
juice.

The simplest crust to make is
the one given in the recipe,
but a crust made with white or
whole wheat flour is delicious,
and tiny Quiche Lorraines can
be made with it to serve as
appetizers. Be sure their crust
is browned on the edges and
crisp.

So many combinations and
variations! Let yourself go and
have fun and make this dish
a delightful surprise every
time you serve it!

entrees

EGGS

Here are a few things about eggs you may not have discovered—especially if you are a younger, less experienced cook.

The whites of eggs have very little flavor. Their mission in cookery is to bind things together or lightly hold other ingredients. Their main value, then, is their viscosity, their stick-togetherness. This capacity is enhanced, when they are being beaten, by the addition of small amounts of salt or sugar. (Never flour or anything of that dry nature which has to be reconstituted.)

Even a tiny drop of any oil, or a bit of the yolk with its high oil content, may prevent their being whipped satisfactorily.

When a recipe calls for whipping both the yolks and whites, I add the salt of the recipe equally to each and whip the yolks first. Yolks have a much heavier body and so hold up longer, and it takes longer

124

to whip them. They should be beaten until they are lemon colored.

The whites whip in less time and will not hold up very long, so they should be whipped just before they are to be folded in. A folding motion should always be used, to incorporate even more air in them and thus counteract the loss of air during the mixing process.

The yolks, having less lightness, yet have most of the flavor that is in the egg, and add richness to everything containing them.

SOUFFLE SECRET

I believe I have discovered a way of easily making souffles that do not collapse immediately as they are removed from the oven. I had thought that the thickness of the white sauce was what held the souffle up, but now I think the way the yolks are handled is the secret of controlling the structure. The yolks should never be

heated before they go into the oven. They should not be added to the white sauce until it is cool. Then, about 1/3 of the beaten whites are stirred into the egg yolk-cheese sauce mixture. Adding some of the beaten whites in this way thins the mixture without making it so juicy that it goes to the bottom when it is poured over the rest of the beaten whites and gently folded in.

As the souffle bakes, the thickening of the yolks establishes the structure and lightness, and produces the wonderful brown hat that appears. The tendency to collapse seems to be practically eliminated.

For the cheese souffle recipe given here, we use a 2-quart pyrex casserole with a slight flair, so that the sides are not straight up and down as are the traditional souffle casseroles. The souffle rises about half of the depth of the bowl. The usual test is to insert a knife, and if it comes out clean the souffle is done.

SPOON BREAD

Spoon bread is actually a corn
meal souffle, and when properly
made is almost as light (taking
into consideration the coarse
texture of corn meal) as any
other souffle.

I have found that yellow corn
meal is too heavy in texture for
spoon bread. The white corn meal
is by far the better. Prepare
this exactly as you do any other
souffle, adding the egg yolks
when the corn meal mixture
is cool.
Scald:
1 quart milk
Add and cook until thick:

**1 cup white corn meal (yellow
will not do)**
2 tablespoons butter

Cool until only lukewarm,
then add:
4 egg yolks, lightly beaten
1 teaspoon salt
Beat until stiff, then add by
folding into mixture:
4 egg whites
3/4 teaspoon salt
Turn into deep greased baking
dish and bake 45 minutes at 400°.
If fresh corn is available, use
2 cups scored and scraped corn
and 1/2 cup white corn meal.
Serves 8.

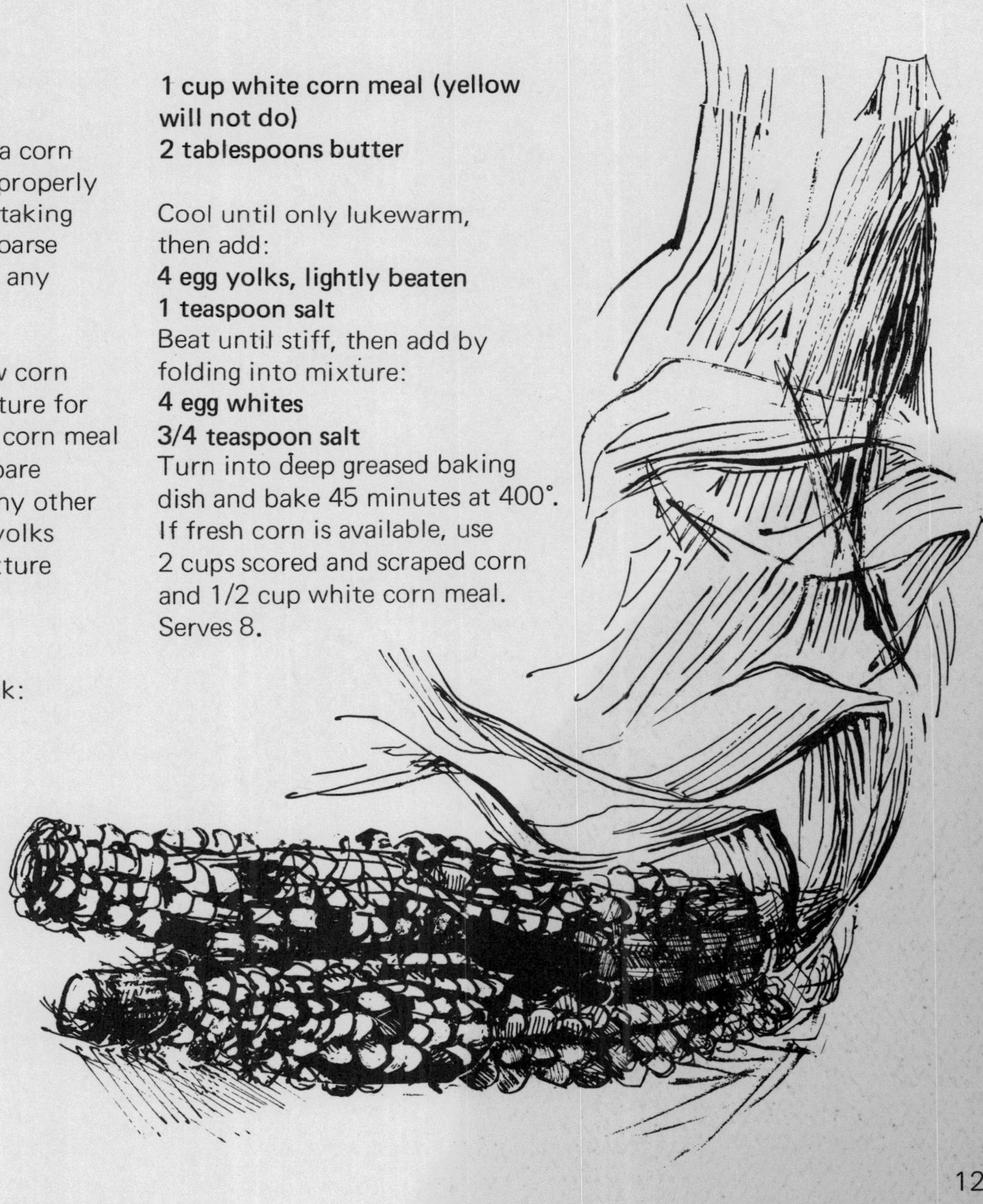

SPINACH SOUFFLE

Heat in pan:
3 tablespoons butter
3 tablespoons flour
When melted and combined, add
and cook until thick:
1 cup milk
**1/2 cup cooked spinach, drained
and chopped**
1 pimiento, chopped (optional)
1/2 teaspoon herb salt
When cool, add and stir in well:
6 egg yolks
Beat until stiff:
6 egg whites
1/2 teaspoon salt
Mix 1/3 of whites into spinach
mixture, folding in. Turn this
mixture into the rest of the
whites and fold in gently. Bake
in ungreased dish for 45 minutes
at 350°, or until knife comes
out clean. Serve with cheese
sauce. Serves 4.

CHEESE SOUFFLE

Melt together in saucepan:
3 tablespoons butter
3 tablespoons bread flour
Add, and stir in well and cook
until thick:
1 cup milk
Then add:
**1/2 pound grated cheese, aged
cheddar or Swiss**
Cool this mixture, then beat in:
6 egg yolks
**1/2 teaspoon Worcestershire
sauce**
dash of cayenne
Whip until very stiff:
6 egg whites
1/2 teaspoon salt
Take 1/3 of whites and fold into
the cheese mixture; then add
the mixture to the rest of the
beaten whites, folding it in
gently, just enough to
incorporate it. Turn into
ungreased baking dish and bake
at 350° for about 45 minutes
or until a knife comes out
clean. Serves 4.

CHEESE SOUFFLE
WITH TAPIOCA

This recipe came from a very
dear friend, Phyllis Calley, who
says it is a never-fail recipe.

Cook until thick (10 minutes):
1-1/2 cups milk
4 tablespoons minute tapioca
Add and stir until dissolved,
then cool to room temperature:
**1 cup sharp cheddar cheese,
grated**
Add and stir in well:
6 egg yolks
**1/2 teaspoon Worcestershire
sauce**
good dash cayenne
Beat until stiff but not dry:
6 egg whites
1/2 teaspoon salt
Fold part of the egg whites
into the cheese mixture, using
a rubber scraper, and then add
this to the remaining beaten
whites. Fold in gently, being
careful not to stir too much.
This method is best for a light

texture. A few bits of unmixed
whites do no harm.

Set in a pan of hot water and
bake at 350° until a knife
comes out clean. Serve at once
with a light cheese sauce and
chopped parsley. Serves 4.

LAZY SUSAN SOUFFLE

Spread lightly with butter and
then mustard and cut into cubes:
5 slices white bread
Put bread cubes in a casserole,
then mix together and pour
over it:
4 eggs
3 cups milk
1 pound cheddar cheese, grated
1/8 teaspoon herb salt
**1/8 teaspoon Worcestershire
sauce**
dash cayenne
Bake at 375° for one hour.
Serve with a light cheese sauce
or a light tomato sauce.
(Page 16). Serves 4.

MUSHROOM SOUFFLE

Stew until tender; then drain
and save juice:
2 tablespoons butter
1/2 cup minced celery
Saute (no water); then drain
and save juice:
1 tablespoon butter
1 quart mushrooms, chopped
Make roux with:
4 tablespoons butter
6 tablespoons flour
Add to roux:
2 cups liquid—juice from celery
and mushrooms plus enough milk
to make required amount
Cook until thick, then add:
1/2 cup cheddar cheese, grated
1/4 teaspoon paprika
1/4 teaspoon MSG (optional)

When sauce boils, stir in
celery and mushrooms; then cool
and stir in:
6 egg yolks
Whip stiff but not dry:
6 egg whites
1/2 teaspoon salt
Add 1/4 of the egg whites to
mushroom mixture and fold in;
then pour the mixture over the
rest of the whites and fold in.
Bake in ungreased casserole
45 minutes at 350°. The
ungreased baking dish allows the
batter to cling to the sides as
it rises and helps prevent
falling after the souffle is
baked. Serve immediately.
Serves 8.

EGGS FLORENTINE

Cook in very little water for
about 5 minutes:
4 bunches fresh spinach
2 teaspoons herb salt
Drain, and spread on bottom of
baking dish, about 1-inch deep.

Make 8 depressions at even
distances in the spinach, and
fill with:
8 raw eggs, one in each hole—
do not break yolks
Melt and mix together:
4 tablespoons butter
4 tablespoons flour
Add and cook until thick:
2 cups milk
1/2 teaspoon salt
Spoon white sauce over spinach
and eggs, and sprinkle over
the top:
grated cheddar cheese
Bake 1/2 hour at 350° or
until egg whites are set. If
yolks are to be hard, bake
longer. For added flavor, add
chopped green peppers or
pimientos to sauce. Serves 8.

OMELETTE, WITH TWO FILLINGS

For omelette for each person,
beat together:
2 eggs
2 tablespoons cream
dash herb salt
Heat pan with:
1 teaspoon butter
Pour in eggs, turn flame down;
cook quickly, lifting edges to
let egg run underneath. When
almost done, spoon filling on
one side, lift the other half
over it, and cook a bit more
until brown.

For mushroom filling, saute:
1 tablespoon butter
1 cup chopped mushrooms
1/4 teaspoon herb salt
Add and thicken:
2 tablespoons Gravy Quick, and
2 tablespoons cornstarch,
dissolved in
10 tablespoons water

For Spanish filling, cook
for 4 minutes:
1 large onion, chopped coarse
4 stalks celery, chopped coarse
1 green pepper, chopped coarse
1/4 cup parsley, chopped fine
a little water
Add and reheat:
3 pimientos, cut coarse
1 teaspoon salt
1/2 teaspoon each, basil
and marjoram
1 cup tomato paste
2 tablespoons sugar
Depending on the number of
omelette servings, you may find
that you have some of the
filling left over. Both of these
fillings can be kept in the
refrigerator and used the next
day. Here are a couple of
suggestions. The mushroom
filling is delicious added to
scrambled eggs or butter-steamed
onions and served over toast as
a luncheon dish.
Both fillings make a fine
addition to vegetable stew, or
mixed with cheese and baked
in a casserole.

entrees

EGGS LILI KRAUS

One day when we were having luncheon in the kitchen of the old Ranch House, in walked a beautiful woman with long black braids hanging down her back—it was Lili Kraus! She was giving a series of concerts at the Happy Valley School, and they sent her to us.

How many times I have cooked for her! She used to practice at the school and then come over famished, wanting something "quick and good." She especially liked the flavor of green peppers with eggs, and so between us we concocted the omelette given below, which I named for her because it was due to her that we have it at all.

Cut up fine and fry in butter:
1 green pepper
1 green onion, including tops
2 fresh mushrooms
dash of omelette herb blend
Beat together:
2 eggs
2 tablespoons cream
dash of herb salt
dash of herb blend
Heat butter in small frying pan until it is very hot. Pour in egg mixture and when it begins to brown, lift up the edges so the liquid will run under and cook. When the eggs are almost done, spoon the mushroom mixture on, sprinkle with grated cheddar cheese and put under the broiler until it puffs up and begins to brown. Serve immediately on a hot plate, sliding it gently from the pan.

ENGLISH EGGS

Allowing one or two for each serving, prepare:
eggs, hardboiled
In a bowl mix enough of the following medium thick cold sauce to cover the eggs:
mayonnaise
cream or evaporated milk
few drops of vinegar or lemon juice
prepared mustard to taste (optional)
Peel the eggs and drop them into the sauce. Garnish with finely chopped celery, green onions or parsley, or finely shredded carrots. In serving, spoon plenty of the sauce over the eggs. Serve accompanied by a salad or as part of a buffet luncheon.

EGG FOO YUNG

Wash and chop:
1 cup parsley
1/2 cup green onions, tops
and bottoms, cut fine
1 large green pepper, cut in
long fine strips
1 bunch watercress tops
(optional)
1/2 cup celery tops
1 cup water chestnuts,
sliced rather thick
1/2 cup bamboo shoots,
sliced thin
1/2 pound fresh bean sprouts
Beat separately:
8 egg yolks—1/2 teaspoon salt
8 egg whites—1/2 teaspoon salt
Fold yolks into whites.
Add from sifter:
8 tablespoons flour
Fold in gently, with only enough
strokes to incorporate
completely. Fold egg mixture
into chopped vegetables.

The batter is the only difficult
part of making this dish. Always
put the salt into the egg yolks
and whites before whipping them.
This will help make a light
batter. The yolks should be
thick and lemon colored when
whipped, and the whites stiff
but not dry, or they will
partly curdle when the yolks are
added to them, and no more
volume will be obtained. The
flour should be added by using
a small sifter, and folded in
with a wire whisk, as in making
angel food cake batter.

All that remains is to add the
chopped vegetables, folding
them in lightly with few strokes.

Heat peanut oil in large skillet
or deep griddle so that batter
dropped in will sizzle around
edges. Drop in a large tablespoon
of batter for each cake. Spoon

oil over cakes to seal them.
Turn with large spatula aided by
spoon, flipping gently. Brown
on both sides. If this is done
correctly there will be no
splashing of the batter at the
edges of the cakes. Don't worry
about the vegetables getting
done; they will cook just
enough if the oil is the right
temperature.

Serve with the following sauce
spooned over the cakes. Serves 8.
Put in saucepan:
1 quart water
1 teaspoon savita, or
1 vegetable cube
4 tablespoons soy sauce
Thicken with:
6 tablespoons cornstarch (no
flour, as this is a clear sauce)
Put 3 cakes on each plate,
lapping one over the other, and
spoon over them the hot sauce
mixture. Serve with rice.

entrees

TOFU WITH TEMPURA VEGETABLES

This makes a good change-of-pace meal. Purchase at a Japanese grocer's:

tofu (bean curd made from soya bean milk)
Chinese cabbage leaves
Prepare:
mushroom sauce (page 15)
Add:
chopped cabbage leaves
Drain tofu and cut into cubes. Fold gently into mushroom sauce so it does not break up. On one end of a platter put a mound of rice, any type; on the other end place the tofu in mushroom sauce: pile rows of
tempura vegetables (page 133)
between, and serve.
Have handy a bottle of soya sauce for those who wish it. What an adventure in texture and flavor is in store for you!

AMERICAN STYLE TEMPURA VEGETABLES

I was asked to create recipes calling for the use of Kikkoman soy sauce (page 181) and this is one of them, a deceptively simple recipe because the end product is so delicious in flavor and interesting in texture. Prepare vegetables thus:
**cauliflower, break into buds
carrots, peeled, cut into
half-inch wide strips
green peppers, cut in strips,
half-inch wide
onion rings, about
one-half inch wide
yams or sweet potatoes—peeled,
cut into half-inch thick slices
zucchini—cut into half-inch
slices**
Put in blender and whirl or whip briskly for three minutes:
**2 eggs
1/4 cup water
1/4 cup Kikkoman soy sauce
3/4 cup white flour**
(Whole wheat flour can be used for more interesting texture. If used, add a very small amount more water.)

Heat in skillet to 375°:
peanut or other frying oil
Fry vegetables one kind at a time. Put enough for one frying into the batter and coat well, then lift out with a strainer and drop into hot oil. Fry until brown. Zucchini and green peppers take the least amount of time; carrots, eggplant and sweet potatoes take longest. Cook the vegetables to suit your taste, soft or textured inside, crisp outside. Drain on paper towels. Keep warm and serve quickly to retain crispness. Serve with buttered rice or other cereal.

RATATOILLE

All through the middle East this dish will be found. There's a legend that the first time it was prepared for a shah he became ill from its richness. We would probably say that the illness came from too much olive oil— the Turkish version calls for twice as much as is given in this recipe. And often the vegetables are over-cooked.

Find, if you can, the long, thin aubergines (eggplant). The usual large eggplant will do. Cook until soft in:
**4 tablespoons olive oil,
2 cloves garlic, chopped.**
Add and continue to cook very slowly until well done:
**2 green peppers cut into
wide strips
2 shallots, chopped (scallions
will do)
1 large eggplant, cut in cubes**
or 2 or 3 small ones, sliced.
Do not peel them.
**1/4 teaspoon basil
1/4 teaspoon thyme
1/4 teaspoon marjoram
pinch rosemary
1 teaspoon salt
1/8 teaspoon pepper
4 tomatoes, quartered, or
1 small can tomato paste**

Cook very slowly in a covered pan. Cook the vegetables to mushiness or leave them with some texture as you choose; I like it both ways. Serve with steamed millet (page 93) or with rice or lentils prepared plain. Don't overeat—it is easy to do!

133

entrees

A TYPICAL INDIAN CURRY

My introduction to real Indian curry was at the Theosophical Headquarters in Wheaton, Illinois. Betsan and John Coats— of the English Coats cotton family—had just returned from India where they had been living for some time. Betsan, who is a tremendously vital and inventive person (and incidentally now has a very successful restaurant in Australia), decided she would prepare a genuine Indian dinner, complete with barefoot girls in saris to serve it.

In order to create as nearly as possible the atmosphere of an Indian restaurant, she cleared the cement-floored basement dining room of furniture and, with washable paint, decorated it with beautiful and typical designs of India. Diners sat on the floor and the food was served on leaves and was eaten with the fingers.

Those who could, sat in Padmasana, the traditional lotus

posture. The others cracked their knee joints trying or just sat as comfortably as they could. The food was brought around in huge dishes by the serving girls and ladled out on our leaves. As no banana trees grow in Illinois, well-washed burdock leaves were substituted. The proper etiquette in India is to pick up the food using only the first two fingers of the right hand. You then flick it off these two fingers into the mouth—and that is quite a trick. I am told that when one drinks from a cup or other vessel in India, the lips are never allowed to touch the vessel. The head is tipped back and the liquid poured into the open mouth.

It was a lovely dinner and all went well until after the finger bowls had been passed, when around came a little box filled with a brown paste. Some of us assumed it to be a dessert and started to eat it, but found it didn't taste so good. It was sandalwood paste, and diners are supposed to rub some on their fingers to remove all traces of the odor of food.

There is no standard recipe for curry. Each cook prefers various combinations, using from a few to fifteen or twenty ingredients to make a single dish. Indians make curry using a "massala" which we call curry powder.

Massala is an Indian word meaning a combination of herbs and/or spices which have been freshly ground together, to be added to onions and garlic which have been "cleared" in "ghee." Ghee is clarified butter. A massala may be used for flavoring many different dishes, each requiring a different combination of herbs and spices. The villagers in India, lacking refrigeration, clarify their butter to keep it from getting rancid. It is set aside in a warm place until all of the solids have precipitated, then the butter oil is poured off. Since it is free from the milk solids which fresh butter contains, this oil has less tendency to become rancid.

A little ghee is put into a saucepan and melted. Onions and garlic chopped fine or coarse are then added and simmered until well done. Then the massala, consisting of the dry, freshly ground herbs and spices is added and this mixture is again simmered until it becomes a slightly thick paste. Heat must be kept low, lest it burn the spices. Fresh coconut milk is then added in the desired amount. A good curry is never thickened with such things as flour or starch. The proportions are gauged so that, after the required number of hours of simmering, it has the correct consistency.

Cow's milk, substituted for coconut milk, doesn't have the same sweet flavor. If it is used in place of the coconut milk, a slight extra sweetening has to be added. A good curry is actually a sweet-sour sauce, combined with vegetables.

Of course there is elaborate preparation involved in the serving of a complete Indian curry dinner, and it always was —and still is for that matter— a major event at the Ranch House.

entrees

RECIPE FOR VEGETABLE CURRY

Put into blender and run until spice is powdered:

2 teaspoons coriander seed (whole)
1-1/2 teaspoon ground turmeric (the whole is too hard)
1/2 teaspoon cumin seed (whole)
1/2 teaspoon mustard seed (whole)
1/2 teaspoon powdered ginger root (the whole is too hard)
1/2 teaspoon pepper corns
2 small red chillis (Japanese type)
1/2 stick whole cinnamon, cut up
2 cardamon seeds, whole but cut in two
1/2 teaspoon Fenugreek seed (whole)
3 cloves, whole

Fry slowly until clear, without browning:

2 tablespoons butter (ghee)
2 cloves garlic, minced
1 cup onions—minced

When onion mixture is clear, add prepared spice mixture. (This is the massala.) Cook for about 30 minutes, very slowly to avoid burning or sticking. When

136

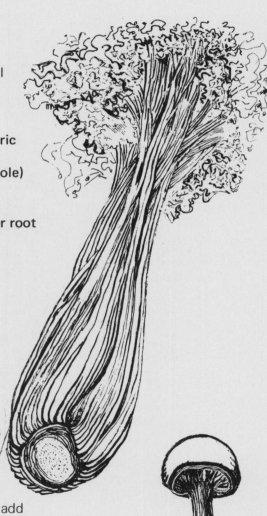

finished, it should be a thick paste. For a more lusty flavor, this spice and onion mixture may be doubled.

Add to the spice and onion mixture, and simmer again very slowly:

2 cups fresh coconut milk

(This can be purchased in many good food shops, frozen fresh or it can be made by using a cup hot water and 1/2 cup coconut meat and running in the blender for 5 minutes and then straining.)

When all ingredients are cooked to a fragrant paste and thinned by the coconut milk and simmered again, add the following cooked vegetables:

1 cup green beans, cut up
1 cup lima beans (do not overcook)
1 cup squash (zucchini, yellow crookneck or green summer)
1 cup celery, cut coarse
1/2 cup carrots—fine slices
1/2 cup cauliflower, small buds (do not overcook these)

Simmer again for about 15 minutes to blend ingredients, then add:

1 cup uncooked fresh or frozen green peas

3 pimientos, diced—fresh cooked or canned
3 or 4 tablespoons lemon or lime juice (to taste)
4 or 5 tablespoons marmalade of some type (orange is good)
Simmer again for about 5 minutes, to blend. Adjust seasoning with salt. Fresh, coarsely shredded coconut may now be added (1/2 cup) and for extra flavor 1/2 cup commercial sour cream stirred in well.

The secret of this type of cooking is to do it slowly on very low heat. Fast cooking will destroy the texture as well as the flavor. Even with all of the cooking, if done properly the vegetables will still have body. Remember, the curry should be sweet-sour in taste, and spicy. For real curry lovers double the red chilis and pepper corns in the curry powder mixture when preparing it.

Rice should always be served with the curry—plenty of it— preferably saffron flavored. Turmeric may be substituted to color and flavor the rice. For a simple curry dinner a vegetable sauce or dahl should always be spooned over part of the rice. Small bowls of yogurt, chutney, peanuts, raisins, coconut (grated or shredded), and cashews should be passed to put on the plate to be delicately mixed with the curry. Cold buttermilk as a beverage is good to take down the heat if the pepper mixture is doubled.

In India, a legume is used to make the dahl which is not readily available in this country, and so I have substituted the nearest thing to it, which is yellow split peas. When finished, this dish should be a semi-thick gruel. In India, I am told, it is eaten in many homes three times a day over rice. This is their main source of protein. As many of the people in India do not eat flesh or even eggs this is a dietary necessity.

DAHL OF YELLOW SPLIT PEAS

Boil gently without covering, until tender but not overcooked:
3/4 cup yellow split peas
2 cups boiling water
1 teaspoon salt
Fry in pan with tight lid, until clear but not brown:
2 cups minced onions
2 tablespoons butter (or ghee)
Make a massala by grinding together:
1-1/2 teaspoons curry powder. (See page 141)
pinch dry mustard
1/2 teaspoon sugar—white
1/2 teaspoon turmeric
Add to the cleared onions and cook to a paste, slowly.

Add the onion and spice paste to the cooked peas, and cook again for about 15 minutes. Remember, slow cooking is the secret.

The dahl should be just thin enough to run down into the rice when spooned over it. Serve with minced parsley sprinkled over the top.

entrees

SAMBALS

Many countries on the other side of the world serve food that is similar to the curried foods of India, and most of them serve it accompanied by a variety of relish and condiment "sambals." These are fresh vegetables and fruits, sliced and marinated in a dressing of seasoned and thickened, cold, fresh coconut milk. Also, a variety of nuts and raisins are passed as dry sambals to be mixed with the curry when it is eaten. It is of great importance that the fruits and vegetables be crisp and fresh before each is marinated in the dressing, and each is marinated separately, never together.

Prepare the following fruits and vegetables and marinate them individually in the chilled dressing: (use enough to just coat each piece but not enough to make them soggy.)
thin sliced peppers—red and green go well together
thin sliced cucumbers
thin sliced red cabbage
tomato wedges—small ones

cooked shoestring beets
hard boiled eggs cut into lengths and then in halves
peeled orange slices cut in halves
Serve in a compartmented dish lined with red lettuce (bronze). For the remaining sambals—dry variety—use:
raisins and almonds fried together in butter until just brown—
do the almonds first and then add the raisins
roasted cashews
peanuts
pine nuts
pistachio nuts
fresh grated coconut
slivered almonds
chutney
yogurt

Poppadums are available in many gourmet food shops. They come packed in small boxes and are prepared by dropping them quickly in very hot oil and taking them out just as they finish curling and before they get a chance to burn which they do easily. These are a very good accompaniment and serve as bread with the curry.

SAMBALS DRESSING

Fresh frozen coconut milk from Hawaii and perhaps other places is now available in many good markets. If none is found near you it can be made as follows:

Put into blender:
4 ounces (1 cup) grated coconut
1 cup very hot water
Run blender for at least 5 minutes to extract all the milk. Press out the milk through a sieve—about 2 cups.

Heat together in saucepan:
2 cups coconut milk, mixed with
2 tablespoons cornstarch
1-1/2 teaspoon onion salt
1/6 teaspoon garlic salt
1/6 teaspoon MSG (optional)
Bring to boil while stirring all the time with wire whip.

When thickened add and stir in well:
4 tablespoons lemon or lime juice
Refrigerate immediately and cover to keep from forming a thick scum on top.

138

If you want to make a green and red hot sauce to accompany a mild curry, for those who like it hotter do as follows:

GREEN HOT SAUCE

Put into blender and run
1 minute:
5 drops green coloring
6 cooked and peeled long green chilis (canned will do)
1/2 cup water
2 tablespoons cornstarch
1 teaspoon vinegar
Put into saucepan and cook slowly until just thick.
Refrigerate.

RED HOT SAUCE

Put into blender and run for 5 minutes until powdered:
1/2 box Japanese chilis
Add and cook until thick in saucepan:
1 cup water
10 drops red coloring
1 tablespoon cornstarch
1 teaspoon vinegar
Serve sauces in small dishes.

Now you will have what is called 18-boy curry. Traditionally, each separate thing should be carried by a small boy in a turban. You can create quite a festive atmosphere if you can find 18 small boys to serve, and persuade them to wear turbans!

A friend of ours who traveled in the East some years ago tells me that in a large hotel in Java, she remembers a 70-boy curry.

entrees

PINEAPPLE
GUAVA CHUTNEY

Many good chutney recipes are
available and here is mine.

Cook to good consistency—nice
and thick; slowly:
3 pounds peeled and halved
pineapple guavas
3 pounds white sugar
1 ounce garlic, minced
1 ounce red chilis, pounded
until they are fine or run in
the blender dry for about
5 minutes. This latter is
easier.
4 ounces fresh sliced ginger
that has been scraped
Add and cook again for
about 30 minutes:
2 cups vinegar
1-1/2 pounds seedless raisins
2 teaspoons salt
1 teaspoon cinnamon,
powdered
1/6 teaspoon cloves
1/6 teaspoon cardamon,
powdered
3/8 teaspoon cayenne pepper
For extra tartness, add
1/2 cup lemon or lime juice

When Beatrice Wood, a well-known ceramic artist from Ojai, went on her first tour of India, sponsored by our government, giving talks on art in the various cities I asked her to buy me some saffron. It never occurred to me to tell her any certain amount although I knew a little about the price of it from previous purchases. When it was convenient she asked her hostess whether her cook could buy some for her. The hostess asked her how much she wanted and she said, "oh, about three pounds." This caused the hostess and the cook to gasp, as its price per pound is about the same as gold. In this country the powder sells at $2.00 for 1/16th of an ounce. She did bring back a small amount for which I was extremely grateful. Indian saffron is richer, darker in its red-orange color, than the Spanish or Italian, and gives a better flavor to rice. A little of the saffron should always be steeped in hot water ahead of time and used as part of the liquid. The following recipe is one prepared in the Indian manner.

SAFFRON RICE

Heat in frying pan that can be tightly covered, preferably a copper clad variety: The 8" size will hold it:
1 cup white rice (unwashed)
2 tablespoons butter (or ghee)
1 teaspoon salt
Melt butter over low heat. Add rice and salt. Stir constantly with wooden spoon until rice begins to absorb butter and turn white. Do not brown it. Now add quickly:
1-1/2 cups boiling water
1/2 cup boiling water in which has been steeped 1/8 teaspoon saffron.
The secret of this method is in having the rice hot enough so that when the boiling water is added it does not stop boiling—otherwise the rice will be gummy and sticky instead of fluffy. Cover it immediately and cook for about 20 or 30 minutes—then keep warm until ready to serve.

On no account remove the lid or stir the rice while it is cooking. As it cooks the grains of rice swell and rise up in the pan forming a structure with holes between the grains. If it is stirred this structure is broken and the rice grains stick together forming a soggy mass. Put an asbestos pad under the pan which should be over the lowest heat. When it is correctly cooked there will be little craters in the surface of the cooked rice.

CURRY POWDER

Grind together in a blender for at least 5 minutes:
2 teaspoons coriander seeds (whole)
1/2 teaspoon cumin seeds (whole)
2 cardamon seeds, cut in half (whole)
2 whole cloves
1/2 teaspoon powdered mace
1/6 teaspoon powdered allspice
1 bay leaf, cut up very fine
3 sprigs fresh thyme, or
1/6 teaspoon dry
1 teaspoon fenugreek seeds (whole)
2 teaspoons turmeric, powdered
2 chilis, Japanese type

entrees

CHEESE ENCHILADAS

Here is our way of making enchiladas. This recipe will serve four people.

Have prepared:
8 tablespoons ripe, pitted olives, chopped
8 tablespoons cheddar cheese, coarsely grated
Pour into 12-inch frying pan:
peanut oil and margarine, half and half, 1 inch deep (oil only, may be used)
Heat, but do not allow oil to get too hot.

Have ready to slide into hot oil:
8 tortillas
Using kitchen forceps, gently slide, separately, four tortillas into the oil, one under another so that the first one stays on top. This will prevent overheating, which would cause them to have bubbles and break apart when being rolled. They must be hot enough to bend easily, but should not start to cook. Remove each tortilla with forceps, allowing each to drip over oil. Stack at the end of
142

a long (1-1/2 x 9 x 13) glass or metal baking dish. Do 4 more and add to stack.
On the tortilla at the top of the stack, put a heaping tablespoon of olives and one of cheese, spreading them in a long line so that the tortilla can be rolled around them as if it were a cigarette paper.
I ran into difficulty when I first tried this. I couldn't get the tortilla to wrap around the other ingredients in the neat roll—like little crepes— and I went back to the grocer to complain. Fortunately, a Mexican woman was there, and helpfully told me that the thing to do was to put the tortilla in hot fat or oil before trying to roll it; and of course this was the proper thing to do to make them pliable.

As the tortillas are rolled, lay them in a row crosswise along the dish. Each should have enough filling so that it is at least an inch in diameter when rolled. The 8 should just fill the baking

dish, with a little room between each one. Dip heated sauce (see below) over them, enough to cover.
Bake at 325° only long enough to get them good and hot all through. They should bubble at the edges of the pan, but should not be cooked too much as the tortillas will become mushy and fall to pieces and the texture will be lost. They should be firm when served, so that the fork can be nicely pressed through them.
Take up the enchiladas with a long, wide spatula aided by a large spoon. Usually, two is a serving. Spoon over each some of the hot sauce and garnish with grated cheese and a green ripe olive. Some like to serve a small pickled yellow hot chili on a toothpick in each enchilada. This is for those who like very hot Mexican food and would think the meal incomplete without the extra hot relish. Onions, very finely chopped and, if desired, mixed with a little chopped parsley, are served in a relish dish and spooned over the enchiladas at the table.

Some cooks prefer to roll the onions inside the enchilada, but I think they lose their extra fresh taste when they are used this way. This freshness is so important to give a lift to the rich heaviness of the enchiladas. Serves 4.

ENCHILADA SAUCE

Put in kettle and bring to boil:
1 No. 2-1/2 can red chili sauce (Ortega Brand)
1 can water
2 vegetable cubes
1/2 teaspoon oregano, pulverized (fresh, if possible)
1/2 teaspoon powdered basil (1 teaspoon, if fresh)
1/6 teaspoon cumin seed, powdered
2 large sprigs fresh silantro
Thicken with:
3 tablespoons cornstarch, dissolved in a little water
Cook until soft and add, but do not boil again:
3 tablespoons grated cheddar cheese
If a hotter sauce is desired, use only 3/4 can of water in making the sauce, and reduce the starch by 1 tablespoon.

entrees

CHILI RELLENO

Bring to boil and keep hot:
1 large can tomato juice
1 bay leaf (discard when cooked)
1 vegetable cube
dash onion salt
dash garlic salt
2 sprigs silantro
Prepare per person:
**1 fresh or canned green
chili pepper**
If canned chilis are used, just
remove the seeds if desired. If
seeds are left in, it will be
a very hot dish. If the chilis
are fresh, place them under
broiler until skin turns brown,
remove and wrap in a cold wet
cloth. Skins will then peel off
easily. Remove seeds if desired.

Cut into pieces 1-1/2 inches
square by 1/2 inch thick;
1 square for each pepper:
cheddar cheese
Wrap the cheese with the whole
chili if it has been seeded. If
left whole with seeds, stuff
cheese into the larger end.

Separate:
1 egg per person
Add to yolks and to whites:
144

1 pinch salt for each egg used
(This will thicken the eggs
and make the batter hold up.)
Measure:
**1 tablespoon sifted flour
per egg**
Beat yolks separately, until
light yellow and thick. Beat
whites until stiff but not dry.
Fold yolks into whites,
then fold flour into egg
mixture, using wire whip. Do
this folding very gently.
Dip wrapped chilis into egg
batter. Lift them out with a
spoon, with sufficient batter to
completely cover each chili, and
fry in hot peanut oil until
brown on one side. Baste before
turning, to keep them from
coming apart and splattering.
Use a spoon and pancake turner
to turn them. They may have to
be turned once again. When light
brown remove and drain on paper
towel. (Peanut oil will not
smoke and burn as quickly as do
other oils.)
Just before serving, immerse
the chilis in the hot tomato
sauce and serve immediately with
additional sauce if desired.
Garnish with grated cheddar
cheese and parsley.

ANOTHER CHILI RELLENO

Slit open and lay on cutting board. (Remove seeds if your palate is sensitive):
12 whole chilis, canned or fresh roasted
Cut into lengths, about 3-1/2 x 1/2; and wrap in chilis:
12 pieces cheddar cheese
Lay these in baking pan, then mix using a wire whisk, and pour over chilis:
4 tablespoons coffee cream
4 tablespoons white flour
4 eggs
dash herb salt
Sprinkle on lightly, to give texture:
sunflower seeds, hulled
Bake at 400° for about 40 minutes. Serve with or without cheese sauce garnished with chopped parsley. Serves 4.

PIMIENTO RELLENO

Drain:
1 can pimientoes
Cut into wedges that will just fit into each pimiento:
mild cheddar cheese
Allow two stuffed pimientoes for each serving. Lay them in a shallow pan.

Mix in blender a batter to pour over the pimientoes, allowing for each four pimientoes:
1 egg
1 tablespoon light cream
1 tablespoon white flour
dash herb salt
1 green onion, including top, chopped
Pour batter over stuffed pimientoes, sprinkle with pine nuts, and bake at 400° until batter rises and is nicely browned. Serve with cheese sauce.

FRENCH FRIED PIMIENTO RELLENO

Stuff, as in previous recipe:
8 canned pimientoes, with mild cheddar cheese wedges
Mix together in blender:
3 eggs
9 tablespoons all-purpose flour
3 tablespoons cream
1/2 teaspoon herb salt
Heat 1/2 inch of oil in a small skillet. Dip stuffed pimientoes into batter and slide them into the hot oil. Fry until golden brown. Do not have the oil so hot that they brown before the cheese melts. Serve on a heated platter, with a mild cheese sauce. Serves 4.

145

entrees

FROM PUERTO RICO

A friend of ours from Puerto
Rico, Isabel Biascoechea, is a
splendid cook of typical Puerto
Rican—or rather, Spanish—food.
She says Spanish food is never
hot, but is very colorful.
Here are four of her recipes.
One, hallaca, is a bit difficult
to prepare and is done in banana
leaves. Isabel said it is
traditional in Puerto Rico and
is sold on street corners in
every town, the way hamburgers
are here.
The oil used in cooking the rice
in this recipe is made with the
seeds of the achiote tree,
native to Puerto Rico.
I understand that most of the
yellow coloring used in foods
is derived from the seeds of
this tree. It is nutritionally
very high in vitamin A.
The little chilis used are sweet
but not hot. The culantro leaves
are available, as far as I know,
only in Puerto Rico, but if you
are an enterprising herb
gardener, you will have coriander
growing in your herb garden and
it can be used as a substitute.

HALLACA—STUFFED BANANA LEAVES

Cook until tender, drain and
save liquid:
1 cup water
1 potato, peeled and cubed
2 stalks celery, sliced thin
2 carrots, diced very fine
1 teaspoon salt
Cook until the corn leaves the
sides of the pan:
liquid from above
8 ears sweet corn, grated
from cob
3 tablespoons achiote oil
(or peanut oil)
1 teaspoon salt
When done add:
8 ounces slightly cooked peas
Saute:
2 tablespoons peanut oil
1 green onion and top, minced
1 clove garlic, minced
When half cooked, add
and cook for 10 minutes:
1/2 green pepper, chopped coarse
1/2 cup canned tomatoes
1/4 teaspoon oregano
1 teaspoon tomato paste
6 sliced, pimiento-stuffed olives
(I always add a little basil,
but Puerto Ricans are
superstitious about this herb.)

Combine all ingredients and mix
well. Take wide banana leaves
and slit out the center vein,
being careful not to tear the
leaves. Cut leaves into 12-inch
sections and wash well, being
careful not to tear them. Lay
each section flat and fill the
center with 4 tablespoons of the
vegetable mixture. Pull the
sides together and fold down
from the top twice to make a
snug fit over the vegetables;
tuck the ends under. Using
colored string (the Puerto
Ricans like to make it colorful),
tie from both sides, making
a rectangular package. Drop the
packages into boiling water and
boil for 15 minutes. Remove
from water, cut the string, and
serve immediately so that when
the leaves are opened the
contents can be eaten while
they are still hot. Makes
12 packages, serving 6 persons.

GARBANZO BEANS

Soak overnight:
1 pound garbanzo beans
Cook slowly, covered with
water, until tender. Do not
finish with too much water so
that beans are mushy. If
pressure cooker is used, cook
at 15 pounds for 35 minutes.

Cook in covered pan:
2 tablespoons cooking oil
1 large onion, minced
Pound in mortar and add to
onion:
1/2 teaspoon salt
1 clove garlic, minced
1/2 teaspoon oregano
1/2 teaspoon basil
2 aji dulce (small Puerto
Rican chilis)
2 culantro or coriander leaves
Add:
1 cup canned tomatoes, mostly
pulp
1/2 bell pepper, chopped
1 cup banana squash, grated
(optional)
1 cup shredded Swiss chard
1 tablespoon olive oil
Combine all ingredients and
cook slowly for 15 minutes.
Serves 6.

entrees

RED BEANS

Soak overnight:
1 pound red beans
Cook until done, about 1 hour,
then add after cooking to
golden brown:
1 cup onions, chopped fine
2 tablespoons cooking oil
Pound in mortar and add to
beans and onions:
1 teaspoon salt
1 clove garlic, minced
1 bell pepper, chopped fine
1 tablespoon Bakon yeast
1 teaspoon oregano
1/2 teaspoon MSG (optional)
Add to mixture:
1 tablespoon tomato paste
1/2 potato, grated
Mash part of beans to thicken
liquid, then cook again very
slowly (they will burn easily
now) for 15 minutes, to cook
the potato. Serves 6.

PUERTO RICAN RICE

Put in small pan:
1 cup peanut or corn oil
2 heaping tablespoons
achiote seeds or a
large pinch turmeric
Heat until seeds boil for
1 minute. Overcooking will
destroy the color. Cool enough
to pour into heated glass jar,
straining off seeds. The oil is
now ready to use.

Heat (not too hot), in frying
pan with tight cover:
2 tablespoons olive oil
Add, and cook slowly until
clear:
1 large minced onion
While onion is cooking,
pound in mortar to pulp, then
add to onion:
2-1/2 teaspoons salt
1 clove garlic
1/4 teaspoon oregano
2 fresh culantro or
coriander leaves
2 fresh sweet chilis, small

1 bell pepper, chopped fine
1/4 teaspoon MSG (optional)
1/4 teaspoon basil (I use
this anyhow!)
Cut into small pieces and add:
1 No. 2-1/2 can tomatoes
When mixture cooks down until
not too watery, add:
2 cups unwashed brown or
white rice
5 stuffed olives, chopped
Cook on high flame until rice
begins to stick to pan, then
add and stir in thoroughly:
4 tablespoons achiote oil
Add:
4 cups boiling water
Cover immediately; turn heat to
simmer; cook until rice is done
without removing cover.
(California brown rice will
require about an hour for
cooking; Louisiana or Texas
brown, or white long grain,
about 1/2 hour.) Serves 8.

ZUCCHINI AND SPAGHETTI

Slice lengthwise then broil
slowly until brown:
zucchini, 4 to 6 inches long
Be sure they are broiled
slowly enough so that they are
thoroughly cooked but not
mushy. Lay the broiled halves in
a baking dish and cover with
slices of provolone cheese. Bake
in 400° oven until cheese
is melted. Serve with
**rich spaghetti, sprinkled with
Parmesan cheese, grated**

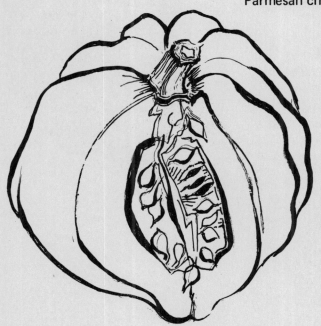

BALLS FOR SPAGHETTI

Braise slowly:
**1 large onion, chopped fine
1 clove garlic, chopped fine
1 teaspoon herb blend
1/4 teaspoon MSG**
Grind:
1 can Choplets
Add to choplets:
**1 can vegetable burger
1/2 cup bread crumbs
1/2 cup rolled oats
2 eggs**
Add onion and garlic mixture
and stir well together.

Make into balls and fry, turning
so that all sides will be evenly
browned. This is difficult to
handle; but if the mixture is
made up too dry the end result
will also be too dry.

entrees

ZUCCHINI ITALIANO

In harvesting zucchini from your garden, sometimes you will miss one of those long green, fat goodies until, when it is discovered, it seems too large to pick and cook in the usual way. But all is not lost—in fact, you have a treat coming. Just let it grow until it gets to be about a foot and a half long, then pick it and wash it well.

Now your only problem is finding a vessel large enough to cook it in. A canning kettle is usually adequate. Cut the zucchini lengthwise and remove the seeds and membrane. Put it in the kettle with about an inch of water and steam it until it is just a bit soft. Don't overcook, as you are going to bake it. Set aside to cool.

Prepare:
cooked spaghetti
cut in 2-inch lengths
Combine spaghetti with:
Italian sauce (page 16)
Place in a long baking pan, cut side up:
the two halves of zucchini
150

Stuff the halves with the spaghetti and sprinkle lavishly with:
Parmesan cheese, grated
Bake until it bubbles nicely around the edges of the spaghetti.
If you want a richer dish, mix some of the cheese into the spaghetti before stuffing the zucchini. In any case, be sure there is plenty of good, sharp cheese for the oil of the cheese should sink into the meat of the zucchini to give the desired flavor.

Place the long green boats on a serving platter and garnish with well-buttered noodles that have been tossed with chopped pimientoes and herb salt. Cut across in large slices and serve with some of the noodles.

FETTUCCINI ALL' ALFREDO

In Rome I had the great pleasure of dining at Alfredo's fine restaurant in the Piazza Augusto. (This is the authentic Alfredo's; there are now several imitators in different places in Rome.) Alfredo showed me all through the kitchen. I met his charming sisters, each one at a cash register checking the food as it left the kitchen, and watched his chef prepare their famous fettuccini.

Stacked in one corner of the kitchen were wicker baskets with a cloth over each one, containing the noodles. They are made in Alfredo's own noodle factory, he told me, where six women work at making noodles. The chef took a three-quart saucepan, filled it about two-thirds full of water and added a little salt. When it was boiling he put in a big handful of noodles—and his hands were unusually large with huge thick fingers. The noodles were boiled about 10 minutes then taken to a sink nearby and drained. Out of a wooden tub the chef scooped a handful of sweet butter and put it on a warm platter. The drained noodles were mounded on the platter and on top of them he put a tremendous handful of grated cheese; Alfredo called it pecorino. I have never found it here in a cheese shop. It is a little stronger than Parmesan but not at all bitter. When Alfredo tosses it in the dining room the result is not stringy but very buttery and cheesy.

As you may know, Alfredo makes a real production out of serving this, his most famous dish. It is brought in on the long white platter and Alfredo comes with a large spoon and fork to toss the noodles very deftly so that the butter and cheese are thoroughly mixed with them. The noodles are then divided among the guests and the large platter on which the fettuccini was served is always given to the most glamorous lady in the party. Long ago Mary Pickford and Douglas Fairbanks dined at Alfredo's, had the fettuccini, and later sent him a gold fork and spoon. Now, when VIP guests come they may use this gold fork and spoon. I was delighted to be thus honored. (By this time they probably have many duplicates for the tourist trade.)

With an ordinary wooden fork and spoon and some practice you can serve with a flourish an American style fettuccini. Follow Alfredo's method, using:
**fettuccini noodles, boiled
10 minutes
sweet butter, plenty of it
at room temperature,
Parmesan cheese, grated,
be lavish with it.**

151

entrees

CANNELLONI NOODLES

Mix together:
1-1/2 cups flour, pastry type
1 teaspoon salt
Make a well in it in a bowl
and add:
9 egg yolks
It can be done with a long fork
stirring the yolks into the
flour being careful not to get
the eggs on the sides of the
bowl. Be sure the mixture is
completely mixed and if in doubt
take out of bowl and knead on
a floured board until it
feels smooth.

An alternate method of mixing
which I find is easier: I use
a Kitchen Aid mixing machine and
put the flour in the mixing
bowl making a well in the flour.
Then add the egg yolks carefully
and by hand with the flat beater
—not the wire whip—gently mix
the flour and egg yolks. When
it is rather well incorporated

put the beater in the machine
and finish the job. This gets
all the egg yolks into the flour
without losing any on the sides
of the bowl.
Turn the dough out on a floured
board and cut it in four even
pieces. Pat it out elongated in
size and with a rolling pin
begin to roll it thinner and
thinner. It should be as thin as
paper and about 4 inches wide
and very long. With a sharp
knife cut the long piece to the
desired width you want the
noodles. Let them dry in a
wicker basket so they will have
plenty of air circulation. Boil
them until done in salted water
and then drain them before
serving.
These noodles do not have to be
dried before using—they can be
rolled out, cut and put at
once into the boiling water.
They should be boiled about
10 minutes then drained.

Here is a dish which is quite
simple and easy to make once you
have prepared cannelloni noodles.
I first had it in one of the
food stalls at the famous Farmers
Market in Hollywood, California.

MANICOTTI

Prepare wide cannelloni noodles
for this recipe. Each noodle
will be filled and rolled into
a "little muff" as the name
of the dish implies.

For the filling, mix well
together:
1 pound ricotta cheese
1/4 teaspoon basil
1/4 teaspoon marjoram
When the noodles are cool enough
to handle spread some of the
filling at one end and roll the
noodle up. Place the filled
noodles in a baking dish folded
side down. Make a light sauce
by pressing the juice from:
canned tomatoes
Add a sprinkling of:
basil and oregano
Pour over noodles and heat in
the oven until just hot. Do not
boil or they will disintegrate.
Serve immediately with a green
vegetable. Serves 4.

GNOCCHI RECIPE FROM ITALY

A friend of ours went to live in Italy, learned the language well enough, she said, to joke with her servants and get from them the following recipe; which she says is the way to make real gnocchi:
Mix and bring to boil:
2 cups milk
2 cups water
Add, stirring constantly, and cook until mixture sticks to spoon:
2 cups Seminola
Spread on a platter to about a half-inch thickness and let it cool. Cut into rounds about the size of a sherry glass. Put the rounds in a baking pan and add:
melted butter
Parmesan cheese, fresh grated

Bake at 350° until golden brown.
If desired a sauce made as follows may be added:
Cook and put through strainer:
fresh tomatoes
Add:
basil and salt to taste.

GNOCCHI ALLA ROMANA

Bring to boil in a saucepan:
1 quart milk
Add, stirring constantly with a wooden spoon:
1/2 pound Farina
Cook for about 10 minutes until mixture thickens. Remove from fire and add:
3 tablespoons grated Parmesan cheese
3 tablespoons melted butter
2 egg yolks, beaten
pinch of salt

Combine thoroughly and pour mixture on buttered platter. Smooth out to about 1/2 inch in thickness. Let stand for several hours, then cut into diamond shaped or round sections. Put a layer in a buttered baking dish and sprinkle with:
Parmesan cheese, grated
Make another layer and sprinkle with cheese. Pour a little melted butter over all and dust again with cheese. Bake in hot oven until lightly browned, about 15 minutes.

I had this dish in London at the Ritz, accompanied by braised celery and endive, broiled tomatoes and artichoke hearts. Delicious! Later we had it at a very famous French restaurant, accompanied by a light tomato sauce. They called it Gnocchi alla Romano.

entrees

HUNGARIAN STYLE HERB NOODLES

Mix well together:
3 cups cake flour
1 sprig of each, basil, thyme, marjoram, costmary and chives, chopped very fine.
3 large sprigs parsley, chopped fine
1-1/2 teaspoons Calumet baking powder
3/4 teaspoon salt
Add, and mix to consistency of cornmeal:
2 tablespoons butter
Make a well in the flour mixture and add:
6 eggs, well beaten
Mix well to make dough.

Have ready a kettle of boiling, salted water. Put about one-third of dough on a floured board and roll it out into a thin sheet. Roll up the sheet and cut across in slices about two-thirds of an inch wide. Roll and slice all of the dough. Unroll the slices and drop them, several at a time, into the boiling water and cook about 5 minutes. (If all are put in at once the water will stop

154

boiling and the noodles will not be as good.) If the noodles are to be kept a while before serving melt plenty of butter in a pan of adequate size, add the noodles and shake them around until they are coated with the butter. This will prevent their sticking together and they can be kept for as long as an hour before serving. Serves 6.

HUNGARIAN NOODLES AND COTTAGE CHEESE

Cook together until just done but not mushy:
1/4 cup butter
1 cup onions, sliced thin
1 clove garlic, minced
Mix together and add:
1 pound creamed cottage cheese
1 pound sour cream
1 teaspoon herb salt
The cottage cheese and sour cream coming from the refrigerator will have cooled down the mixture. Add:
Hungarian noodles
and mix well together, then warm again, only to serving temperature. More will make the cheese stringy. Serves 6.

YOLANDA'S CASSEROLE

This recipe is named for a warm-hearted friend who is also a marvelous cook.
Prepare:
Hungarian Herb Noodles
Put in cooking pot with
1/2 cup water:
1 quart green beans, French cut.
The long thin ones are best.
Spread over beans:
1 large onion, sliced thin
1/2 teaspoon savory herb blend
1 teaspoon herb salt
Cook until just done, then drain. Generously butter a medium sized casserole. On the bottom put a layer of noodles, then a layer of the cooked beans and onion, then make a layer of:
small spoons of cottage cheese
small spoons of sour cream
thin slices of Philadelphia cream cheese
Continue these layers until the baking dish is filled. Top with sour cream and a good sprinkling of paprika. Bake at 350° until it bubbles, and serve immediately. The heartiness depends on the amount of cottage cheese used so govern yourself accordingly. Serves 6.

NOODLES AND SPINACH

Boil 9 minutes:
**1 pound medium cut noodles,
in 3 quarts water**
When done drain and put into
long, shallow baking dish.

Cook damp enough so that extra
water will not have to be
added:
1-1/2 pounds spinach
When done, add:
4 vegetable cubes, mashed
Grind:
1 teaspoon onion salt
1/2 teaspoon garlic salt
1/4 teaspoon MSG (optional)
1/2 teaspoon savory herb blend
1/2 teaspoon celery seed
Add to spinach along with:
1-1/2 cups light cream
Stir well and spread over
noodles in baking dish, then
cover with:
6 ounces grated cheddar cheese
Press cheese down. If it is
allowed to stick up it will
brown too much and not form the
desired light crust on top of
the noodles. Bake until cheese
is melted and crusted lightly.
Cut with large spatula and serve
with shoestring beets, buttered

carrots or other vegetable of
bright color. This is a famous
recipe served at the coffee shop
of the Sherman Hotel in Chicago.
Serves 8.

NOODLES MEXICALI

Cook in salted water until
tender:
**1/2 pound noodles—semi-broad
variety**
Braise in pressure cooker,
without cap, for 3 minutes:
2 tablespoons butter
1 teaspoon salt
2-1/2 cups celery, cut coarse
2-1/2 cups onions, cut coarse
**3 cups green peppers,
cut coarse**
Grind in mortar; then add
to vegetables:
1 teaspoon herb salt
1/4 teaspoon basil
1/8 teaspoon marjoram
Make white sauce with:
2 tablespoons flour, mixed in
2 tablespoons melted butter
Add and cook until thick:
2 cups milk
Put layer of 1/2 of cooked
noodles in large baking dish.
Cover with 1/2 of cooked

vegetables, salted lightly. Lay
on strips of:
cheddar cheese
Add:
**1/3 cup green chilis, with
seeds removed, cut up**
Add:
1/2 of white sauce
Repeat another layer, as above.
Bake at 350° for about 1/2
hour, until it bubbles well.
Serves 6.

155

desserts

DESSERTS

Cookbooks have so many wonderful desserts, one would think there is hardly a need for more; still, some of the recipes given here may titillate your palate. Many are my own creations, often made at the request of customers who have come to the Ranch House so frequently that they have become good friends, and I love nothing better than to try to find new things to delight them.

Most families have handed down to them or they originate recipes that are made over and over again for the enjoyment of family and friends . . . Mothers are famous within their circle for these charming tastebud pleasures, and rightly so. In our family many such treasures came from an old, coming-to-pieces little brown book kept by my grandmother from about 1860. Ingredients were called for in scant cups, heaping teaspoons, etc., as was the custom before the advent of Fannie Farmer of Boston Cooking School fame who revolutionized the whole system of measures in recipes. Her insistence that all measures be level and exact has been a great boon, especially to those just learning the fine art of cooking.

There is good reason for my interest in food, an awareness of the opportunities for creating an atmosphere of gentle good will. A kind of thankfulness for the blessings of good food and companionship enhance my memories of our family life when I was young. We seemed always to have family friends at our table, especially for Sunday dinner. Dad was the meat cook for these occasions and of course Mother did the pastries. My sister Dorothy took care of the table arrangements, and I had a hand in the salads and vegetables.

During the roaring twenties I was a pianist playing in jazz bands and away from home most of the time. On holidays and especially on my birthdays Mother always remembered me by mailing one of her famous Imperial Sunshine cakes. She would get just the right sized box, wrap the cake in wax paper, put a small bunch of flowers in the center, and send the package off special delivery. It was amazing how it always arrived in such good condition. She would write on the package, "Handle with care—special birthday cake!" Perhaps this legend stayed the throwing hands of postal employees. Here is the cake:

IMPERIAL SUNSHINE CAKE

Follow the directions exactly. Have all ingredients measured and the flour sifted as directed. You will need these ingredients:

1 cup cake flour
3/4 teaspoon cream of tartar
1-1/2 cups white sugar
1/2 cup water
6 eggs, whites and yolks beaten separately
1/4 teaspoon salt, added to egg whites before beating
1 teaspoon orange extract

Sift the flour once, measure out one cup, add cream of tartar and sift again three times. Boil sugar and water until it threads when dropped from the tip of a spoon. Pour the hot syrup in a fine stream on the beaten egg whites, beating mixture until cool. Now add the well-beaten egg yolks. Fold the flour very carefully into the egg mixture, and mix in the orange extract. Pour into an ungreased angelfood cake pan and bake 50 to 60 minutes in a moderately slow oven (325 to 350°). When done, invert to cool. Do not ice this cake! The flavor and texture are too marvelous to be diluted by anything.

desserts

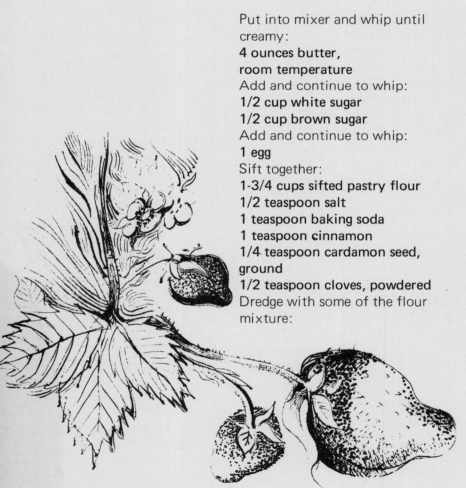

APPLESAUCE
SPICE CAKE
(Old Wives Tale Cake)

Put into mixer and whip until
creamy:
4 ounces butter,
room temperature
Add and continue to whip:
1/2 cup white sugar
1/2 cup brown sugar
Add and continue to whip:
1 egg
Sift together:
1-3/4 cups sifted pastry flour
1/2 teaspoon salt
1 teaspoon baking soda
1 teaspoon cinnamon
1/4 teaspoon cardamon seed,
ground
1/2 teaspoon cloves, powdered
Dredge with some of the flour
mixture:

1/2 cup raisins
1/2 cup currants
Add remaining flour mixture to
batter and incorporate:
1 cup applesauce sweetened
lightly, strained and slightly
warm
Add to mixture and beat well:
dredged fruit
1 cup chopped walnuts
Bake in greased tube pan at 350°
for 50 minutes. Ice with brandy
cheese icing.

BRANDY CHEESE ICING

Whip until very creamy,
5 minutes:
2 ounces Philadelphia
cream cheese
1-1/2 tablespoons coffee cream
1/2 pound powdered sugar
1/4 teaspoon vanilla
1 ounce good brandy

RUM TRIFLE

Use a 9-inch glass casserole that can be tightly covered. Lay **almond macaroons** upside down, on the bottom of the casserole. Spoon over them, dividing it evenly, **1 tablespoon good dark Rum** Myers' "Planters' Punch" is excellent.

Split **8-inch sponge cake** in two even flat pieces and lay bottom half on macaroons. Spread this with **seedless raspberry jam** not too thick. Lay on this jam enough macaroons to completely cover it. Place on this the top half of the sponge cake.

Pour over top half—spreading evenly—
2 tablespoons rum.
Do not do this until ready to pour over it the cooked custard as it will soak up too much and be inclined to be soggy.

Make custard as follows:

Put into top of double boiler:
4 egg yolks
1/4 cup white sugar
1 pinch salt
1 teaspoon vanilla (imitation holds the flavor better because of refrigerating the trifle)

Add:
1 pint hot milk
Heat in double boiler, stirring constantly, until custard coats a tablespoon.

Pour immediately over top of cake layers in bowl. Use a tablespoon and pour directly into the bowl of the spoon so that the pouring stream will not make a hole in the cake top. Gently lift up sides of cake so custard will flow into bottom of bowl and soak the macaroons underneath. Cover immediately and refrigerate for at least 24 hours. The finished product should be neither too soggy nor too dry when served. Top should be lightly glazed with the custard.

CALIFORNIA ORANGE-RAISIN CAKE

Grind:
2 orange rinds after juicing
1 cup seedless type raisins
Put into mixing bowl with the following, and beat but not too hard:
1 stick butter
1-1/4 cups white sugar
2 eggs
1 teaspoon salt
2/3 cups buttermilk
2 cups sifted pastry flour
1 teaspoon baking soda
Put into greased loaf pan and bake about 45 minutes at 350°. A tube pan works very well.

Prepare by mixing well:
3/4 cup orange juice
1 teaspoon curacao (optional)
1/4 cup sugar
When cake is done spoon liquid over it immediately, spreading evenly.

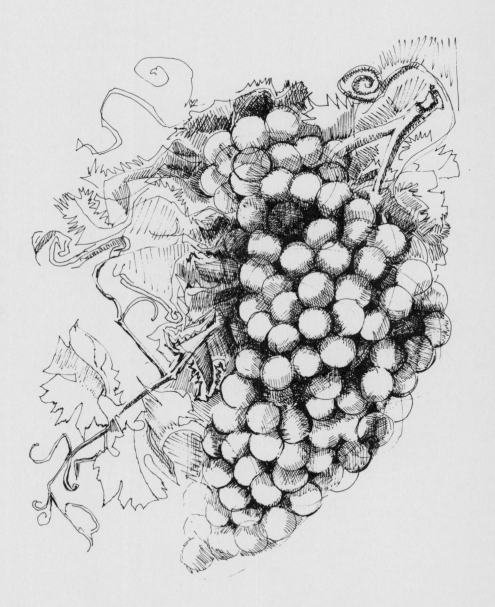

DARK FRUIT CAKE
(This recipe makes six cakes)

Steam for 5 minutes over boiling water:
3 pounds seedless raisins
1/2 pound currants
Cream well:
1 pound butter
Add and mix well, in mixer with whip:
2 cups brown sugar, light type
Add and whip well:
6 eggs, at room temperature
Add and whip well:
1/4 cup molasses
1/4 cup orange juice
1/4 cup sherry
2 tablespoons vanilla
4 tablespoons white Karo syrup
Sift together and then whip in:
5 cups bread flour, white
1-1/2 teaspoons cinnamon
1/2 teaspoon cloves, powdered
1/2 teaspoon nutgeg
1/2 teaspoon allspice
1/2 teaspoon mace
1/2 teaspoon baking soda
1 teaspoon Calumet baking powder
1/2 teaspoon salt
Put raisins and currants, while still hot, into a large pan.

Add and mix together:
3 pounds mixed candied fruit, diced
1 pound glace cherries
1/4 pound pitted dates, chopped
Add and mix well:
1 cup flour
This will keep the fruit from settling to the bottom of the cake batter.
Add to the candied fruit, then mix all into the cake batter:
1 pound chopped walnuts
1/2 pound chopped pecans
Divide into 6 foil pans.
Decorate tops with
cherries, almonds, walnuts and pieces of candied pineapple.
Bake at 250° for about 2 hours. The tops will rise and crack slightly when the cake is done. Remove from oven and glaze with:
3/4 cup white Karo syrup mixed well with
2 teaspoons water
When cakes are cool, bend the sides of the foil pan away from the cake and pour over each side:
1 tablespoon brandy
replace foil sides of pan, cover and store to age.

SOFT GINGER BREAD

Cream together:
1 cup butter
1 cup sugar, white
Mix well together and add:
2 teaspoons baking soda, dissolved in
1 cup boiling water
1 cup molasses
1 teaspoon salt
1 teaspoon ginger
1 teaspoon cinnamon
2-3/4 cups white flour
Mix all ingredients well together, then add and beat in:
2 eggs
Pour into greased 9x13-inch shallow baking pan.
Bake at 350° for about 45 minutes or until a straw inserted comes out clean. Ice with a mixture of:
thin milk and powdered sugar
When cool this gingerbread can be sealed in a plastic bag and frozen. To defrost, it only needs to be removed from the bag and put in the oven for about 20 minutes at low heat and it is as good as new. A wonderful idea for the busy working cook.

desserts

ALMOND BUND CAKE
GERMAN KUCHEN

Dissolve in 1/4 cup of
lukewarm water:
1 cake yeast
1 teaspoon sugar
Heat to lukewarm and add yeast
mixture:
1 cup milk
Mix in large bowl:
1 cup butter, room temperature
1 lemon rind, grated
1/2 cup sugar
pinch salt

Beat and add:
4 egg yolks
When yeast mixture is frothy,
add:
1 cup bread flour, sifted
Combine all ingredients in
mixing bowl and add:
2-1/2 cups bread flour, sifted
Beat well to develop the wheat
gluten. Put into bowl, cover and
store in refrigerator overnight.
Next day, make the following
filling:
Whip to soft peaks:
4 egg whites
pinch salt

Add slowly to incorporate:
3/4 cup white flour, sifted
Add slowly again:
1 cup ground almonds
Roll dough out on floured board
to 1/2-inch thickness, and
spread filling mixture evenly
over dough. Roll up like jelly
roll, into a long roll. Put into
greased tube pan, bringing ends
together to meet and form
a ring. Let rise in a warm
place to double its bulk,
covered with towel to keep it
from forming a crust on top.
Bake about an hour at 350°.

CHERRY NUT CAKE

This recipe makes five medium sized loaves.

Sift together and hold:

5-1/2 cups bread flour
1 teaspoon Calumet baking powder
1/2 teaspoon baking soda
1/2 teaspoon salt
1/2 teaspoon cardamon, powdered
1-1/2 teaspoons mace

Whip in mixing bowl until very light and fluffy:

1 pound butter

must be room temperature.

Add and continue to whip:

2 cups white sugar

Add and continue to whip:
6 eggs, room temperature
Add and continue to whip:
3/4 cup sherry, regular, not dry type
4 tablespoons white Karo syrup
2 tablespoons vanilla
Add and continue whipping until well mixed:
sifted flour mixture
Mix together:
3 pounds cherries
1/2 cup bread flour

Add:
1 pound shelled walnuts, halved
Fold cherry and walnut mixture into cake batter. Be sure all ingredients are well incorporated then divide into 5 medium sized bread pans and decorate the top with
cherries and walnuts.
Bake at 250° for 2 hours and about 10 minutes. The top should rise slightly and crack open when done. Remove from oven and glaze with a mixture of:
3/4 cup light corn syrup
2 tablespoons water

desserts

FOLLIES BERGERE PEACH MELBA

Make a syrup of:
1 cup water
2 cups white sugar
1/4 teaspoon vanilla
Poach for 1 minute in the syrup:
3 pounds ripe peaches, peeled and cut in halves
Lift peach halves from syrup, cool, then chill in refrigerator. (Syrup can be saved for fresh fruit compote.)

Put into mixer and whip well:
1 pound seedless black cap raspberry jam
4 tablespoons brandy
2 teaspoons chocolate sauce
1 tablespoon rich port wine
For each serving put in dessert bowl:
1 scoop vanilla ice cream
1 peach half, pit side down, on top of ice cream
Spoon over ice cream:
2 tablespoons syrup.
Top with:
whipped cream.
Serves 8 or more.

FRESH FRUIT COMPOTE

When peaches are in season, so are other wonderful fruits. Combine whatever you find in the market, something like this:
1 pound peaches, peeled and sliced
1 pound seedless grapes
1 pound apricots, peeled and halved
1 pound pears, peeled and sliced
2 cups melon balls taken from: casaba, crenshaw, honey dew, watermelon
Make a syrup with:
2 cups sugar
1 cup water
Boil in covered pan 5 minutes. Then add:
1/2 teaspoon vanilla extract
With a slotted spoon gently place peaches in syrup and poach until just soft.
Remove peaches and chill syrup.
Mix together:
1/2 cup cointreau
1/2 cup brandy
2 cups syrup from poached peaches

Gently toss the fruit in the brandy sauce and let stand in refrigerator for at least one hour to marinate.

Hollow out one half of the watermelon and chill it. When ready to serve, pour fruit from refrigerator into chilled melon shell. Garnish with:
whipped cream
green and red cherries

BAKED PRUNE WHIP

Put through ricer:
2/3 cup cooked prunes
Add and mix together:
1/2 cup sugar
1 teaspoon lemon juice
Fold into mixture:
2 egg whites, well beaten
1/8 teaspoon salt
Turn into greased baking dish. Put baking dish in a pan of hot water and bake in the oven at 350° for about 45 minutes, until firm.

Serve at once with whipped cream or custard sauce.

PEACH DUMPLINGS

When properly made, these are
light and airy and full of
wonderful flavor.
In a fairly large kettle that
can be tightly covered, put:
**1 large can of sliced cling
peaches and the syrup**
Mix together:
**4 cups pie flour
1 teaspoon salt
8 teaspoons Royal baking powder**
(This is the type that begins
to rise when it is moistened.)
Add and mix until the dough
feels like coarse cornmeal:
1/3 cup shortening
Beat in a 2-cup measuring cup:
**1 egg
milk to make 1-1/2 cups liquid**

Add beaten egg and milk to dry
ingredients and mix only enough
to incorporate: Do not overmix.
Have peach liquid boiling. To
make dumplings, dip a tablespoon
into boiling liquid, then dip
a spoonful of the dumpling
mixture into the pot; dip the
spoon again, and again add
a dumpling, and so on, **quickly.**
Cover the pot immediately. **Do
not remove the cover while
cooking.** It takes about
15 minutes for the dumplings to
cook. Serve peaches, dumplings
and some of the juice in large
soup bowls and add coffee cream.

This is an old southern Ohio
dish that used to be served for
supper.

desserts

CHERRY PUDDING

A tube pan is needed for baking
this pudding. If you do not have
one, you can make a substitute.
Take the tube from a roll of
hand towels, cut it in half and
wrap a half in aluminum foil.
Stand this tube in the center of
a casserole. Voila!

Drain and reserve the juice from:
**1 No. 2 can of sour pitted
cherries**
Butter the tube pan or
casserole-with-tube and cover
the bottom of it with
the cherries.

Cream in the mixer, using the
beater, not the whip:
1/4 cup butter
1/2 cup white sugar
When well mixed, add and
whip again:
2 eggs
Sift together and then beat in:
2 cups pastry flour
**1 tablespoon Royal Baking
powder**
1/2 teaspoon salt
Add and mix again, but do not
overmix:
1/4 cup milk
166

Spread the mixture over the
cherries and bake at 375°
for 40 minutes. Turn out onto
a hot plate, cut in wedges, and
serve with the following sauce.

Combine and bring to a boil:
**1 No. 2 can of cherries with
juice and juice from first can**
Add and cook until clear
and thick:
**4 tablespoons cornstarch,
mixed well with
1 cup sugar**
When done add and stir in well:
1/2 cup water
Heat to serving temperature and
spoon over the pudding, which
has been brought to the table.
(A handsome sauce boat is
wonderful for this occasion.)

TIPSY PUDDING

And it really is! Some years
ago an English friend who had
a store where I traded gave me
this recipe. She said it was
a great favorite with her
family, and so it may be
with yours.

Break (do not cut) into glass
casserole:
pieces of very stale cake
The cake must be dry and rather
hard so it will absorb:
1 cup of sherry
Soak for one hour.

Heat in double boiler, stirring
constantly, until the back of
a spoon is well coated:
2 cups milk
3 egg yolks, lightly beaten
1 cup sugar
1/8 teaspoon salt
1/2 teaspoon vanilla
Do not overcook or it will
curdle. Pour custard over
soaked cake. Top with:
**whipped cream, sweetened and
generously flavored with rum.**
Serves 6 unless they like
sherry—then only 4.

ELSIE DE WOLF'S SUZETTE PANCAKE BATTER

Mix together:
2-1/4 cups sifted flour
3 eggs
dash salt
Stir in:
1 tablespoon melted butter
1 tablespoon cognac
Set the mixture aside for one hour, then put through a fine sieve. Use a small frying pan, four to six inches in diameter. Grease with melted butter. Drop in a scant spoonful of batter and tip the pan around to spread it evenly. Fry over fairly high heat, browning lightly on both sides. To make the crepes, put your own concoction in the center, fold the pancake over it and fill a chafing dish with them. Add:
melted butter
powdered sugar
Pour over them a small glass of:
rum or brandy
and set aflame.

PERSIMMON CREAM

Audye Reynolds Tuttle, who contributed to the first Ranch House cookbook, gives us another of her wonderful inventions, beautifully simple and delicious.

Run in blender for at least 4 minutes:
2 cups peeled persimmons
1 cup whipping cream
1/2 cup coffee cream
When smooth and thick put in sherbet glasses and chill for at least 1 hour.
Garnish with:
whipped cream
2 tablespoons coarsely chopped pecans (optional)
a drop of red color
may be added to the whipped cream.

167

desserts

MRS. BERGENGREN'S INDIAN PUDDING

Mix together and cook in double
boiler until thick like
a cereal:
1 quart milk
3 tablespoons fine yellow
cornmeal
2 tablespoons tapioca, soaked
soft in water
When thoroughly cooked, add:
1 cup molasses (light preferred)
1 teaspoon cinnamon
1 egg
Mix well, then pour into
buttered baking dish. Bake
2 hours at 275°, covered.
Serves 8. Serve with vanilla
ice cream while still warm.

COFFEE MOUSSE

Mix together and heat in
double boiler:
1-1/2 cups strong coffee
1/2 cup milk
1/3 cup sugar
1 tablespoon gelatin
Beat well with spoon:
3 egg yolks
Pour hot mixture over beaten
yolks, stirring constantly.

Add and beat in only enough to
dissolve, then let cool:
1/3 cup sugar
1/2 teaspoon vanilla
Beat until light and fluffy;
then fold into coffee mixture:
3 egg whites
1/4 teaspoon salt
Pour into sherbet glasses and
chill. Serve topped with
whipped cream.
Serves 6.

FROZEN CHEESE WITH FIGS

Put through a sieve:
3/4 pound cottage cheese
Mix together and add:
2 cups sour cream
1/2 teaspoon salt
1/8 teaspoon nutmeg
1/2 cup sugar
1 teaspoon lemon extract
Turn into refrigerator tray
and freeze.

To serve, have ready:
8 preserved figs
Cut frozen cheese mixture into
squares, place on a lettuce leaf
and arrange a fig in the center
of each square. Serves 8. (Or it
is rich enough to stretch to 10.)

CHEESE PASKHA

This is an Easter sweet, from Russia, pressed in a wooden mold and usually bearing the sign of the Cross or the initials meaning Christ is Risen.

Mix well together:
3/4 pound cream cheese
1/2 cup sour cream
1/4 pound sweet butter
1/4 pound sugar
1/4 pound chopped almonds
1/4 pound mixed orange and citron peel
1/2 pound seedless white raisins
If you have no mold, put the mixture in a cloth and let it hang for at least a day.

ANOTHER PASKHA

Beat until thick and lemon colored:
2 egg yolks
Stir in gradually and beat well:
2 cups sugar
Cream until fluffy, then combine with egg mixture:
1 pound sweet butter
Put through a sieve, then blend into egg and butter mixture:
2 pounds dry cottage cheese
Whip and add:
1/2 pint whipping cream
1 teaspoon vanilla or almond extract
Mix together and fold in:
1 cup seedless raisins
1/2 cup chopped citron, or mixed candied peel
Put mixture in a wet cloth and press into mold. Put a weight on top and chill in refrigerator for two days. To serve, turn out of mold and remove cloth carefully, then slice.

PRALINES

Using candy thermometer, cook for 3 minutes at 240°:
4 cups brown sugar
1/2 cup coffee cream
2 tablespoons butter
Remove from heat and stir in immediately:
1/2 pound pecan halves (not pieces)
Wait until the candy has begun to cool slightly and then put a spoonful on waxed paper to see if it has cooled enough to begin to set. It should crystalize when cold. If it is spooned out too soon the first few will stay sticky and cannot be removed from the paper.

desserts

MOCHA WALNUT OR HAZELNUT TORTE

Put into mixing bowl and beat
2 minutes scraping down bowl
at least twice:
3 cups sifted pastry flour
1-2/3 cups sugar
1/2 cup + 1 tablespoon shortening
1 teaspoon salt
4 teaspoons Calumet baking powder
1/2 the liquid below
Liquid: The cold milk is
warmed by the hot water; it
should not be hot when put
into cake:
6 ounces milk, from refrigerator
2 ounces very hot water
1 teaspoon vanilla

Add remaining milk mixture and
beat for 1 minute scraping down
bowl. Put into blender half at

a time and run until nuts are
ground fine:
1-1/2 cups walnuts
Fold in walnuts gently.

(Variant: Do the same with
1-1/2 cups hazelnuts but when
using them 1/4 cup more water
has to be added for they are
a much dryer nutmeal.)

Line a sheet cake pan 11-1/2 x
17-1/2 with wax paper. Spread
batter evenly in the pan and
bake at 350° for 25 minutes.

When cool turn cake out on board
and with long knife cut it twice
lengthwise, evenly and once
across to make 6 long pieces.
Then split each piece twice to
make three layers. They are then
put together with **mocha icing**
so that each one has 6 layers.

The icing must be soft enough so
that when it is spread it will
not pull the crumbs from the
middle layers of the pieces.
Nuts may be spaced on top of
each one for decoration. They
may be wrapped in foil and
stored in the freezer for they
keep that way very well.

MOCHA ICING

Melt together and mix well:
1/2 square chocolate
2 ounces butter
Beat in mixer until very light:
1-1/2 pounds powdered sugar
7 tablespoons coffee cream
1/2 teaspoon vanilla
1-1/2 tablespoons powdered coffee
When sugar mixture is very light,
add melted chocolate mixture
and mix thoroughly.

CREAM MERINGUE TORTE

Beat until soft:
1/4 cup butter
Sift and blend into butter:
1/2 cup sugar
Blend until light and fluffy,
then beat in:
4 egg yolks
1/2 teaspoon vanilla
Sift together:
1 cup cake flour
2 teaspoons Calumet
baking powder
1/4 teaspoon salt
Add sifted ingredients to butter
mixture alternately with:
5 tablespoons cream
Beat batter until smooth then
spread into 2 greased 9-inch
cake pans.

Whip until stiff:
4 egg whites
1/8 teaspoon salt
Add slowly and mix in:
1 cup sugar
Fold in:
1 teaspoon vanilla
Spread meringue carefully over
both layers in pans. Stud one
meringued layer with:
1/3 cup blanched and shredded
almonds
Bake in slow over (350°) for
about 40 minutes. Remove from
oven and cool in pans. Shortly
before serving place the layer
without almond meringe side
down on a cake plate. Spread on
it, reserving 4 tablespoons:
cream or custard filling (page 174)
or whipped cream
Place almond studded layer,
meringue side up, on cream
filling and spread reserved
filling on top. Garnish with:
strawberries, apricots,
cherries or other fruit

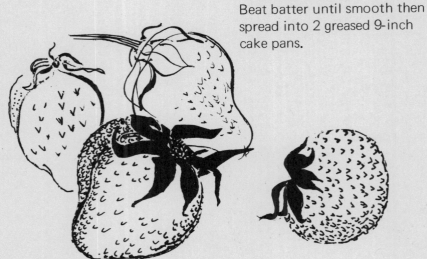

desserts

NEW ORLEANS DELIGHT

Two popular Ranch House menu
items take only egg yolks—Rum
Trifle and Bearnaise sauce.
There was the problem of what to
do with all those egg whites.
We solved it by making meringues.
So we had a problem: what to do
with all those meringues?
A sauce was devised which had
the flavor of pralines. From
there on it seemed a natural
progression to fill the
meringue with coffee ice cream,
put the praline sauce over it
and then add pecans. Thus was
born one of our most popular
desserts. When we decided to
serve it, I thought how nice
it would look served with a
paper doily under it. It was so
delicious, and it did look
pretty. One Sunday afternoon
I happened to be watching an
elderly lady as she ate her
New Orleans Delight (the
appropriate name we gave it).
Imagine my horror as I saw that
she was eating the doily right
along with the dessert!
I rushed over to her table and
gently pointed out her error.
The dear lady looked up and
said, "It's so delicious,
I don't care!"—and she went
right on eating the doily.
I thought no greater praise
could have been heaped on
anything than that.

MERINGUES

Whip in mixer on high speed
until quite stiff:
**1-1/4 cups egg whites,
room temperature**
3/8 teaspoon salt
Add, while whipping at
lowest speed:
2-1/2 cups + 1 tablespoon sugar
When whipping in the sugar
be sure it is thoroughly
dissolved. If it is not, the
meringues will weep, and not
get crisp and will be tough
on the bottom.

When all sugar is incorporated,
add and fold in gently:
3/4 teaspoon vanilla
Drop each spoonful on a
brown-paper-lined cooky sheet.
Spread into a circle with
rubber scraper or spatula—not
too thick for they rise
a little in the baking. Try
1/2 inch for thickness. If a
pastry bag is used they may be
made into meringue cups by
coiling the meringue up at
the edge of each flat circle
until the desired height
is reached.

Slow baking is essential.
A baker told me that to let
the meringues set for a couple
of hours before baking will
make them whiter in color after
they are baked. Bake at 275° for
55 minutes. Remove from oven
and just when they are cool lift
them from the brown paper. If
they stand too long they are
hard to get loose from the paper.

PRALINE SAUCE

Mix together:
2 cups brown sugar, firmly packed
1/2 cup white Karo syrup
2 tablespoons butter
3/4 cup coffee cream
2 teaspoons molasses, not blackstrap
1/8 teaspoon Mapeline
Using candy thermometer, boil to 220° and then cool. Do not overcook as it will crystalize later.

CREME DE MENTHE SAUCE

Boil for 5 minutes in covered saucepan:
2-3/4 cups white sugar
1-1/2 cups water
3/4 cup white Karo syrup
5 drops green coloring
When cool but not cold, add and stir in well:
3/4 cup green Creme de Menthe
1/8 cup dry sauterne
This sauce does not need to be chilled. If stored in refrigerator it will crystalize.

GREEN GINGER SAUCE

Soak overnight:
1/2 pound fresh ginger root
Next day, scrape off skin and slice thin, then cut into 1/8-inch cubes.

Put into saucepan with lid and boil for 5 minutes, covered:
2 cups white sugar
7/8 cup water
1/4 cup white corn syrup
When syrup is cooked add the cut up ginger and continue to boil *gently* for another 30 minutes. Boil very slowly so the water will not be evaporated. Keep covered while cooking. When done add:
2 or 3 drops green food coloring
This sauce is delicious over vanilla ice cream, topped with grated coconut.

RUSSIAN CREAM SAUCE

Beat together until thick and light colored:
2 egg yolks
3 tablespoons sugar
Add and beat until light and fluffy:
1 cup cream
Stir in:
4 tablespoons rum
Beat until they peak and then fold in:
2 egg whites
Serve over
strawberries, peaches, etc.
Serves 4 to 6.

AVOCADO SHERBET

Mix well together, then freeze:
1 large avocado
lime juice to taste
tangerine rind, grated
lemon juice to taste
3 egg whites, beaten
1-1/2 cups sugar
2 cups water
1 package gelatin

desserts

MERINGUE FOR CREAM PIES

The secret of a good meringue is to have the egg whites at room temperature. This recipe makes meringue for one pie.

Whip until peaks form:
2 egg whites
large pinch of salt
Add and whip only enough to dissolve sugar:
6 tablespoons white sugar
few drops vanilla
Spread on pie and brown at 450° until just brown, 6 or 7 minutes. This makes a tender meringue without drying it out.

CREAM FILLING FOR PIES

Mix in saucepan and bring to boil:
1-1/2 cups whole milk
3/4 cup white sugar
Mix with wire whip and add to hot milk; stir vigorously while cooking until it thickens:
1 cup whole milk.
3-1/2 tablespoons cornstarch
2 egg yolks
1/8 teaspoon salt
1 teaspoon vanilla
When thick remove from heat, add and stir in well:
1 tablespoon butter
Any fruit may be added to this mixture if it is well drained or fresh, such as:
sliced peaches, canned seedless grapes, apricots or figs
Also lightly toasted nuts may be added:
pecans; English or black walnuts; macadamias; cashews

FRUIT TART SHELLS

Makes about two dozen shells.
Mix well:
1/2 pound bread flour
2 ounces stone ground whole wheat flour
1-1/2 ounces brown sugar
1-1/2 ounces raw sugar
1 teaspoon salt
7 ounces vegetable shortening
Add and mix again:
3 ounces cold water
Roll out dough very thin and cut circles that just fit over inverted tart tins. Bake at 375° about 15 minutes. Watch carefully to prevent burning, but shells must be nice and brown. Take from oven and remove shells from tins *immediately* while they are still flexible, to prevent breakage.

PIE CRUST

Follow method carefully. With
two knives, cut:
1 cup shortening
into
2-1/2 cups bread flour
seasoned with
1 teaspoon salt
leaving pieces of shortening
about the size of marbles.
Now with the hands rubbing
together in opposite directions,
sheet the flour and shortening
into flat pieces of shortening
with a thick coating of flour.
Do not overmix! Stop before
you think you should. Make a
hole in the center of the
mixture and pour in
1/2 cup water
Quickly mix together with
a spoon, only enough to enable
you to handle the dough. Again,
stop mixing before you think
you should! Turn the dough out
on a floured board and divide
into halves. Press it out
gently, very gently, and roll
out to the desired thickness.
If mixed right this dough will
make a good thick top crust
for fruit pies without being
tough. The very thin layers

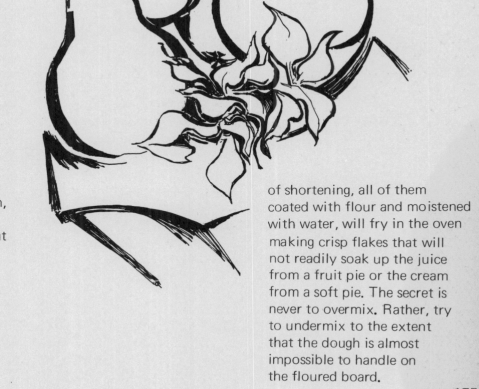

of shortening, all of them
coated with flour and moistened
with water, will fry in the oven
making crisp flakes that will
not readily soak up the juice
from a fruit pie or the cream
from a soft pie. The secret is
never to overmix. Rather, try
to undermix to the extent
that the dough is almost
impossible to handle on
the floured board.

desserts

FRESH APRICOT PIE

Put into saucepan and bring
to boil:
1/2 cup apricot pulp
2 cups water
1/8 teaspoon salt
8 tablespoons cornstarch
Add and bring to boil again:
2 cups sugar
juice of 2-1/2 lemons
pinch of nutmeg
pinch of cinnamon
Add and mix in:
2-1/2 pounds pitted apricots
Fill unbaked pastry shell and
put on lattice top or complete
top as desired. Bake at 450°
for about 25 minutes until
nicely browned.

TOASTED PECAN CREAM PIE

Mix in saucepan and bring
to boil:
1-1/2 cups whole milk
3/4 cup white sugar
Mix together with whip, add to
hot mixture and cook until thick:
1 cup whole milk
3-1/2 tablespoons cornstarch
2 egg yolks
1/8 teaspoon salt
1 teaspoon vanilla
Add to thickened mixture:
1/2 cup toasted pecans
Pour into baked pie shell and
refrigerate immediately, only
enough to completely cool the
filling. Remove and top with:
whipped cream or meringue
(page 174).
If meringue is used, bake at 450°
until brown.

FRESH RHUBARB PIE

Place in kettle and bring
to boil:
1 cup water
2 drops red coloring
pinch salt
Add and cook until very thick.
Do not scorch.
4 tablespoons cornstarch
dissolved in a little water
or 2 ounces Sur-Jel
Add and stir until dissolved:
4 cups white sugar
Add and mix in:
2-1/2 pounds rhubarb cut into
1-inch pieces
Spread in uncooked pie shell
and cover with stripped top or
solid crust. Bake at 450° for
about 25 minutes, until done.

FRESH COCONUT CREAM PIE

Mix in saucepan and bring
to boil:
1-1/2 cups whole milk
3/4 cup sugar
1/2 cup shredded coconut, fresh
Prepare cream-filling mixture
(page 174), add to above and
cook until thick. Pour into
prebaked pie shell and chill.
Top with meringue or whipped
cream. Garnish with grated
fresh coconut.

FRESH PERSIMMON CREAM PIE AND BANANA CREAM PIE

Prepare cream pie filling
(page 174). Slice
persimmons
like orange segments and lay on
bottom of prebaked pie shell.
Pour over segments the
custard filling
and chill immediately. Top with
whipped cream.
If meringue is used, browning
it may make the persimmons too
mushy because of the extra heat.

Use the same method to make
banana pie, putting sliced
bananas in the pie shell. Top
with meringue or whipped cream.

PECAN PIE

Mix together:
2 tablespoons melted butter
1 cup light brown sugar
2 tablespoons flour
Add and beat in:
2 eggs
1 teaspoon vanilla
1/4 teaspoon salt
Add and beat lightly:
1 cup white Karo syrup
Pour into unbaked pie shell and
sprinkle on top:
1/2 cup pecan halves
Bake at 375° for 35 minutes.

desserts

GREEN TOMATO MINCE FILLING

In the mid-west, this is an autumn time recipe, usually made when the first frost may catch the green tomatoes on the vine before they have had time to ripen. Naturally, it can be made any time firm, green tomatoes are available.

Mix in a large kettle:
2-1/2 pounds green tomatoes, cubed
2-1/8 pounds tart, peeled apples, cubed
6 ounces currants
1-1/4 pounds seedless raisins
4-1/4 cups brown sugar
1-1/4 cups vinegar
1-1/2 tablespoons cinnamon
1/2 tablespoon cloves, powdered
1-1/4 teaspoons allspice
1-1/4 teaspoons mace
1-1/4 teaspoons black pepper, ground
1 tablespoon salt
1 pound mixed candied fruit, diced
Simmer for about 3 hours very gently, until apples and tomatoes are cooked. Then mix in:
1/2 pound butter, sliced thin
Store in a tightly covered crock until ready to use. When ready to make pies, mix in:
1/2 cup brandy
1/2 cup sherry

CHEESE CAKE

Mix thoroughly, and while still hot line a glass 10-inch pie baking pan with:
8 graham crackers, rolled fine
2 ounces melted butter
1/4 cup brown sugar
1/8 teaspoon cinnamon
Reserve 2 tablespoons of the graham cracker mixture to sprinkle on top of cake.
Whip in mixer:
8 ounces Philadelphia cheese
4 ounces Hoop cheese (dry bakers variety)
Add and whip more:
3 eggs
Add and whip more:
2 tablespoons lemon or lime juice
1/2 teaspoon grated rind
Add and whip in:
1/2 cup white sugar
4 tablespoons sour cream
Pour into crumb lined pie pan. Bake at 350° for 20 minutes. Remove and sprinkle remaining crumbs on top. Return to oven and bake 6 minutes more—no longer as it will tend to dry out. It should be a little shaky when removed but not too soft in the middle. This cake is soft when cut but not runny.

FUDGE PIE

The temperature of the
ingredients is the secret to
the success of this dessert.

Beat together but not until
fluffy: (do not overbeat this!!)
**1 stick butter, room
temperature**
1 cup sugar
1 teaspoon vanilla
Melt in saucepan and then cool
so it can be poured into mixing
bowl without melting the
butter and sugar mixture:
**2 squares Bakers bitter
chocolate**
Add and beat again:
2 egg yolks, room temperature
Add and beat enough to smooth
out the batter:

1/3 cup flour, sifted measure
Turn into wide mixing bowl.
Beat in another bowl, very stiff:
2 egg whites
1/8 teaspoon salt
When egg whites are very stiff
add, and beat until dissolved:
1 tablespoon sugar
Fold into chocolate mixture the
beaten egg whites and pour into
cake pan that has a built-in
cutter, for this is extremely
difficult to get out of pan
when cold. Bake at 325° for
30 minutes. When cold, serve
with either vanilla, coffee or
peppermint stick ice cream laid
in a thin slice on top.

Idiots' delight—top ice cream
with fudge sauce and then creme
de menthe sauce (page 173)

talk of many things

"The time has come,
the walrus said . . ."
—L. Carrol

There are some things too good to leave out, that seemingly have no specific place in a book like this.

KITCHEN EQUIPMENT

Pressure Cooker So many recipes in this book call for the use of a pressure cooker, a friend said that something should be written about one so that the person unfamiliar with its use might be able to use one easily. There are many types on the market—some aluminum and some made of stainless steel. The former are completely satisfactory but if the price is not too high the stainless variety is easier to clean.

There is little danger in using these pressure pots because the simplest ones have a weighted pressure cap that will quickly tell if the pressure is too high. All that could happen is that the little cap would be knocked off if it weren't attended to in time. We use them without the cap for many vegetables. This way there is still a little pressure built up because of the slowness of the escaping steam.

If the vegetables are to be served with a sauce added later, then place a trivet in the bottom of the cooker and use about 1/2 cup of water in the pot. If they are to be served in their own juice then do not use the trivet—just add the seasoning and butter or olive oil later, after the vegetables are cooked. Remember—one of the secrets of well-flavored vegetables is to use as little liquid as possible in cooking them to prevent the dilution of their own juices.

Gricer A cone-shaped device with cutting holes in it. This either bolts on to the table or has a rubber suction cup that holds fast to a smooth surface. There are usually three cones accompanying it that make tiny threads, shoestring-like threads or thin slices of food. It can be used for shredding cheese, coconut, vegetables, etc.

Rotary Slicer This is a very handy tool but not essential. It consists of a wheel with very sharp blades that rotate against the food to be sliced. It is excellent for slicing cabbage very thin, potatoes, beets, carrots or any other food.

Mixing Machines Many kinds of mixers are now on the market. One of them, the Kitchen Aid, is a heavy duty model and has many different attachments. All of them are useful for their particular work. It is especially handy to have two wire beaters when doing baking to avoid the necessity of constantly washing one of them.

VEGETARIAN FOOD PRODUCTS

Bakon Yeast This product is very good in the normal vegetarian diet and a real flavor boon in the restricted diet for it contains no starch, sugar, meat or salt. It is 100% hickory smoked torula yeast and can be added to anything when a bacon or rich nutty flavor is desired.

Gravy Quick As its name suggests, this is a commercial product of good quality, used chiefly to make gravy; low in calories, made of wheat flour, yeast extract, soy and other vegetable proteins.

Savita A thick paste made of vegetable protein and spices for flavoring vegetarian dishes, used for years by vegetarian cooks.

Vegeburger, Choplets Meat substitutes canned under the Loma Linda brand name, well known to most vegetarians.

Hoop Cheese or soft baker's cheese, obtainable at most dairies. It is actually cottage cheese with a good deal of the moisture removed, too strong in flavor for serving alone but excellent used in cooking.

AMERICAN SYSTEM OF LIQUID MEASURES

Since so many of my friends in England and in Europe have said they want copies of this book, perhaps this little table will be helpful to them:

3 teaspoons	= 1 tablespoon
2 tablespoons	= 1 ounce
8 ounces	= 1 cup
2 cups	= 1 pound
	= 1 pint
4 cups	= 2 pounds
	= 1 quart
8 pounds	= 4 quarts
	= 1 gallon

A RECOMMENDED SOY SAUCE

One has to be alert not to be taken in by a poor substitute for good flavor. I had always thought that all the various brands labelled "soy sauce" were the same substance. Then I was introduced to Kikkoman, which is an authentic *brewed* soy sauce (or *shoyu,* as the Japanese call it). I was surprised and pleased to find how rich the flavor of Kikkoman Soy Sauce is, and how superior to other brands I had tried. My interest was stimulated, and I invented several new recipes using Kikkoman.

An interesting sidelight is that *shoyu* was developed about a thousand years ago when Buddhism, which prohibits meat-eating, was at its height in Japan. *Shoyu* was designed to add flavor as well as protein to vegetarian food.

talk of many things

SUNDAY BRUNCH ON THE HILL

When the Ranch House was still in its original location, and people came in the back way because the front porch was in no condition to hold them up, Sunday brunch was an event that friends brought outsiders to as a special treat. People would come by on their Sunday morning horseback rides, park their mounts under the trees in the back yard, and come in to sit at the kitchen table so they could have sour cream pancakes hot off the griddle.

SOUR CREAM PANCAKES

Put into electric mixer and beat thoroughly mixed:
3/4 pint sour whipping cream (Commercial sour cream can be used but it will not work as well)
1/2 cup whole milk
4 eggs, unbeaten
1/2 cup white flour
1/8 cup wheat germ
1/4 cup whole wheat flour, preferably stone ground type
1/4 cup old-fashioned rolled oats—not the quick-cooking variety
1 teaspoon baking soda
1/2 teaspoon salt
Heat ungreased griddle until batter dropped on it sizzles. Unless the griddle is hot enough, the cakes do not rise quickly and therefore do not attain their real lightness. If it is too hot, they burn before they can be turned. The frying is the most difficult part as it is hard to keep the griddle a bit too hot, rather than too cold. Small bubbles appear when one side is done, but lift up a corner to see when they need turning.

They cook rapidly, and usually are ready to turn before they seem done. They must be handled carefully to avoid splashing the batter when they are turned. Make them small, 2 or 3 inches across, so they can be turned with ease. Larger ones break in the turning since they are so tender.

Because of the tenderness they should never be served with cold butter or syrup. Many prefer just hot maple syrup and hot butter over them but then others, who do not want so much sweetness, like maple butter, which is easy to make.

MAPLE BUTTER

Put into the small bowl of the electric mixer:
3/4 cup butter, room temperature
Whip the butter, scraping down the sides of the bowl, til it is light and like whipped cream.
Slowly thread in:
1 pound maple syrup, room temperature
Whip mixture until light and fluffy.

182

NANCY'S SEVILLE ORANGE MARMALADE

This is the best recipe I have found to make English style orange marmalade. Use only:
bitter, wild oranges
Wash thoroughly the amount of fruit to be used. Cut each orange lengthwise in half. Lay cut side down in a shallow dish and slice very thin, beginning at the stem end of the half. Save all of the juice and the seeds. Put the seeds in a muslin bag. They have the pectin necessary to make the mixture jell. The muslin bag should be large enough to allow the seeds to swell as they cook. To each pound of fruit and juice add:
2-1/2 pints of water
then add:
the bag of seeds

Boil for 10 minutes then let stand a full 24 hours; boil 10 minutes again and let stand another 24 hours. Remove seed bag. Thoroughly squeeze all the pectin from the seed bag into the oranges. For each pint of fruit and juice, add:
1 pound sugar
Bring to boil and continue boiling for at least 25 minutes. Have jars washed and hot. Pour marmalade into them, seal and cool. (Great for Christmas gifts if put into attractive bottles.)

WHOLE CRANBERRY SAUCE

Place in saucepan and boil for 5 minutes:
2 cups sugar
2 cups water
Add and cook without stirring for 5 minutes (longer makes the sauce more firm if that is wanted).
1 pound washed cranberries, well drained
Cranberries will usually pop within 5 minutes. They should all pop to allow the sugar to get inside them.

GRANDMOTHER'S SPICED NUTS

We went to a ranch to get walnuts and the man in charge asked if I would like to taste some spiced walnuts he had just prepared. Naturally I did, and they were a delicious concoction. He said the recipe was a very old one given to him by his grandmother. Here it is:

Combine in a 2-quart saucepan:
1 cup sugar
1/4 teaspoon salt
1 teaspoon sugar
6 tablespoons milk
Cook, testing with thermometer, until mixture reaches the soft ball stage—236°. Remove from heat and quickly stir in:
1 teaspoon vanilla
Stir in quickly and mix well, then spread out on waxed paper:
3 cups walnut halves

Work quickly so that the nuts can be separated before they crystalize into a hard ball. Other nuts are good prepared this way but walnuts are best.

183

talk of many things

DOLMA

Fry lightly in olive oil:
1 can grape leaves. (Fresh leaves are not tender enough. The canned ones may be obtained in any shop where Asian foods are sold.)
Grind:
1 teaspoon salt
1/2 teaspoon dill
1 clove garlic
2 or 3 large mint leaves
3 tablespoons olive oil
1 minced onion
Cook slowly until onion is clear, then add:
1 cup white rice
Heat again and add:
juice of 1 lemon in
2 cups of boiling water
Be sure water does not stop boiling when it is added to rice. If it does the rice will be sticky and the grains will not be separate. Spread the rice mixture on each grape leaf and roll into small long cylinders. Fry these again in olive oil. Refrigerate for at least 4 hours, then serve with Asian food as an appetizer, two or three to a serving. The dolma should be quite tart.

184

FRESH MUSHROOM CANAPES

Wash and slice:
6 ounces fresh mushrooms
Fry them until dry in:
butter
Dredge lightly in:
2 tablespoons flour
Add:
3/4 teaspoon lemon juice
1/2 teaspoon herb salt
dash pepper
5 ounces thick cream, enough to moisten the mushrooms
Mix well and then spread on hot split biscuits which have been well buttered. Run under broiler and toast lightly.

SANDWICH FILLING FOR DATE-NUT BREAD

Put into mixing bowl and whip for at least 2 minutes:
4 ounces Philadelphia cream cheese
1-1/2 ounces orange concentrate, frozen type but thawed
1 tablespoon honey
1/16 teaspoon cardamon seed, powdered

PIMIENTO SPREAD

Whip in small bowl of electric mixer:
8 ounces Philadelphia cream cheese
1/2 teaspoon herb salt
Cut into 1/2 inch pieces and add to mixture and whip only 10 seconds:
4-ounce can pimientos
Do not overwhip this last stage as the spread will get soft.
A variation of this can be made by using one half pimientos and one half canned and peeled green chilis.

ELSIE DE WOLF'S MARBURY ROLLS

Cut in thin slices and butter:
fresh white or sandwich bread
Spread along one side of slice:
chopped or sliced olives
grated Parmesan cheese
Sprinkle with:
paprika and a small amount of cayenne
Roll like a cigarette and fasten with a toothpick. Lay on a baking sheet and brown in the oven just before serving.

RAGLETTE

This is one of the famous Swiss dishes served after a skiing party, everyone sitting around a great fireplace, glass of white wine in hand and spicy conversation flowing. You really need a fireplace for this.

On a stand close to the fire so it will keep warm and soft on one side, have:
1 large square Emmentaler cheese
(The Swiss without many holes)
Have warmed plates at hand. Take off from the soft side of the cheese a very thin slice and place it flat on a hot plate.

Have ready:
**small new potatoes,
boiled with jackets on**
Keep them hot by wrapping them in a cloth. Have them handy in a large wooden bowl.
Each guest should be given a special three-tined fork (the tines are very sharp and in a triangle so the potatoes can be speared without breaking) and a small knife for peeling the potatoes. Cut off a bite of the peeled potato, wrap it in cheese, pop it into your mouth and wash it down with wine! The Swiss potatoes are small and sweet and flavorful, so let this be your buying guide.

SWISS SHISHKABOB

Cut in half:
Gruyere cheese that comes in little foil-wrapped wedges.
Cut in similar wedges:
white bread slices
Thread bread and cheese wedges alternately on small skewers. Dip each one in milk, then in flour, and finally in beaten egg yolk. Fry in deep fat which must be very hot. Drain and serve, plain or with tomato sauce.

talk of many things

YOGURT

You can start making your own yogurt simply by taking a small portion from a carton of any reliable commercial yogurt or, better still, obtain a **live culture** from your health food store. What you are going to do is to provide a situation wherein this culture can grow. To do this you put it in milk and keep the milk at a constant body-heat temperature. It can be put on an asbestos mat over the pilot light of your stove or, if you are dedicated to making your own yogurt you can buy, through your health food or hardware store, an electrical device made to keep the mixture at the correct and constant temperature. If you can get **TB certified raw milk** from your dairy this is the best to use, to assure top quality. Start with a quart of warm milk. Stir in 1/2 cup of the culture. Cover the container with a solid cover, not a cloth, and put it in the warm place. Within 24 hours it should be set, and you can take a half cup of it and start the whole process over again. It is that simple.

Yogurt is not just sour milk. Wonderful bacteria live in it and they help to keep established in the intestines the necessary flora that make digestion possible in the human body. People in Europe and especially people of the near East have eaten yogurt for centuries. Mix it with a little brown or raw sugar and put it over fresh fruit; use it in place of sour cream or with a little jam mixed in; just plain, cool yogurt is delicious.

QUINCE HONEY

Peel and grate:
5 large quince
Make syrup, using:
1 pint boiling water
5 pounds white sugar
Heat but do not boil until sugar is dissolved, then add quince and cook 15 to 20 minutes. If quince is overripe, add
1 teaspoon lemon juice after
after boiling 20 minutes.
Store as you would jelly.

INTERESTING HOT CHOCOLATE

Melt on low heat:
1 square Bakers dark chocolate
Add:
1/2 cup hot water
Mix together and add:
6 tablespoons sugar
2 tablespoons cocoa
1 teaspoon powdered coffee
Then add:
few drops almond flavoring or a little almond paste
Heat nearly to boiling and add:
1 quart whole milk
Reheat to serving temperature.
Whip well with wire whisk.
Top with:
whipped cream or marshmallow

index

index

index

ABOUT THE AUTHOR

Alan Hooker has always been a non-conformist, plunging into life with great enthusiasm. His determination to see for himself, to find his own way, has led him down many paths, and at last to remarkable success as a restaurateur.

Born in a small Illinois village, Alan showed an early preoccupation with travel, food, and hospitality. At three he used to disconcert his mother by inviting passers-by in to dinner. About this time he also made his first culinary innovation. From his usual observation post on a kitchen chair, he "improved" some cake batter with an extra ingredient. This, discovered when the cake was cut, was— a nail.

In college he majored in chemistry, and the disciplines he learned in the laboratory were later of great help in developing recipe formulas for his restaurant and bakery. Out of school, enthusiasm for jazz led him to become a pianist. With jazz orchestras he traveled widely in the United States and Europe, where his lively interest in food took him not only to the best restaurants but usually into the kitchen for a chat with the head chef.

Then, in an about-face, he left the entertainment world to join a communal group engaged in the serious study of Eastern philosophy. There he met his wife Helen; became a vegetarian; and managed a bakery. In this, his first venture into the food field, he created new recipes for breads and pies. These were so successful, plans were made to expand the bakery into a chain, with Alan managing. Appalled at the prospect, Alan resigned. He and Helen fled to California and settled in the lovely Ojai Valley, where he started his now-famous garden restaurant, the Ranch House. On becoming a vegetarian Alan had formulated his own original approach to delicious cookery. Applying this approach to meat and fish entrees as well as vegetarian foods, Alan developed for the Ranch House a menu of unique delights. Seventy-five of the herbs used in its cuisine are grown in the restaurant garden, along with many of the fresh vegetables and fruits. The delectable desserts and breads are baked in the kitchen.

Alan's creative verve continues undiminished. Even with over 500 different recipes now in the Ranch House master formula book, he continues to originate new dishes, seeking and finding the fresh combination, the unexpected meld of tastes and textures, that gives his food its subtlety and savor.